PAINTING ○ COLOR ○ HISTORY

COLLECTION PLANNED AND DIRECTED BY

ALBERT SKIRA

SPANISH PAINTING

FROM
THE CATALAN FRESCOS
TO EL GRECO

TEXT BY JACQUES LASSAIGNE

TRANSLATED BY STUART GILBERT

SKIRA

CONTENTS

THE COLORPLATES

Almost inevitably when we refer to Spanish Painting we have in mind a few great artists—El Greco, Zurbaran, Velazquez, Goya—standing out in lonely eminence, and, even if we vaguely know that from the Middle Ages onward there flourished other Spanish Schools and painters highly thought of in their day, we can hardly bring ourselves to admit that the works of the great artists named above, "the happy few," had a context and were not wholly isolated phenomena. Moreover art historians tend to stress the discontinuity of Spanish art, its abrupt setbacks, its diversions into sometimes sterile byways and the aridity of certain periods during which foreign artists had to be called in to the rescue. All these circumstances conspire to accentuate the seeming isolation of the Masters in any panoramic view of Spanish art.

We do not claim to be able to fill these gaps. Interesting as are the discoveries of specialists in this field, and valiant as are their efforts to resuscitate indifferent painters, these can but tend, in the long run, to confirm our impression of a great gulf between the Masters and the lesser lights. On the other hand, when we confine our attention to works of outstanding quality, we find affinities between them, indeed a very real unity; thus the true aspect of Spanish painting, as an organic whole with distinctive characteristics of its own, becomes apparent. This is why we decided to abandon the idea of presenting in these volumes certain painters whose names figure in every textbook on Spanish Art, when their work did not come up to the exacting standard we had set. We felt the less compunction in so doing because highly interesting works, as yet unknown to all but specialists, are so much more numerous and varied than is commonly supposed. Corresponding to the great diversity of the various art centers there is a no less striking variety of manners in which the creative impulse took effect in Spain. Though it seems unlikely that many wholly new discoveries remain to be made, the identification and regrouping of the known works now in progress is already pointing the way to a general revision of accepted values.

Viewed as a whole, Spanish Art does not give the impression of a continuous, majestic progress—which indeed could hardly be expected considering that no less than six centuries elapsed between the Romanesque painting of Catalonia and the coming of Goya. Italian art, after displaying unbroken continuity of development between the 13th and 16th centuries, showed signs of faltering in the 17th. Flemish and Dutch painting reached their apogee within much shorter periods. It has always been the way of Spanish art to manifest itself as a succession of highlights; its great works emerge suddenly, unconditioned seemingly by Space or Time, and the only obvious link between them is their intensity, a similar and special attitude of their creators towards art and life.

Nothing would be gained by trying to define the Spanish Schools in terms of any foreign Schools, especially those of Italy and the Low Countries. Their courses did not run parallel. Moreover, though inevitably and unquestionably Spanish painters came under foreign influences, these were quickly absorbed by them, assimilated and expelled; indeed, often as not, the remarkable thing is the way the Spanish artist reacted *against* such influences and took the opportunity of asserting all the more energetically his own personality.

Spanish art is, in fact, an art of exceptionally strong personalities and emotional experiences of extreme intensity. Thus though at first sight a work by one of the Spanish

Primitives may strike us as forbiddingly austere and unrewarding, we have only to look at it attentively (or, better still, possess it) to feel its latent power—an experience vouched for by many collectors who, sceptical at first, have soon been won over to a lasting admiration; so potent is the impression such works convey of a compelling presence and the autonomous creative will behind them.

The development of Romanesque art in Catalonia is of particular interest, since even in its earliest days it broke with the impersonal aridity of Byzantine convention and allowed the individual artist scope for self-expression. Stemming from observation of the real world, it did not follow that progress from the abstract to the concrete which we so often observe in primitive arts. The Catalan artist, after annexing the data of visual experience, bent them to his will to synthesis and imparted to them significance and a stylization based at once on their essential characteristics and his own impulse towards abstraction. Thus, throughout successive metamorphoses, this art succeeded in maintaining a grandeur worthy of its highest period.

We find this mastery of forms in the art of Ferrer Bassa, the first Primitive to emerge from the darkness of the 14th century. In his vast decorative compositions this painter gives his figures a wonderfully lifelike suggestion of movement, and his bold simplifications vouch for a remarkable grip of reality combined with a feeling for the inner life of those whom he portrays.

It was a happy inspiration on the part of the Catalan painters when they struck on the idea of transposing the huge mural decorations of the churches to the smaller dimensions of baldachins and altar-fronts, and adapted the technique of the fresco to that of painting on wood. For thus they pointed the way to that art of the retable which was carried to such memorable heights in Spain, and moreover it was due to their pioneer work and its widespread influence that the Primitive Spanish Schools came to exhibit such rich and remarkable diversity. For not only was each School quick to strike out on its own lines, but the work of individual artists within the group, each following his own bent, led to new and often quite unpredictable developments. Despite its expressionist propensities and its fondness for color, Valencian art culminated in an almost static monumentalism, an austere reduction of the picture's content to essentials. In the art of Barcelona, on the other hand, we find a humanistic suavity, a love for all things visible and smoothly rounded forms; yet behind this seeming sensuality we glimpse a mystical vision of reality. In Castile, where Flemish art was much in evidence, artists used the facilities for precise interpretation which the new techniques provided, for expressing the most intimate secrets of the Spanish temperament and landscape. Seldom great colorists, the Spanish Primitives were invariably admirable draftsmen and, though often their artistic means were limited, they showed rare mastery in the handling of them. Accurate drawing, balanced composition, a spare use of tones and a fine sense of texture came naturally to the Spanish Primitive.

During the latter half of the 15th century some great painters, men of wider scope and interests, came on the scene: Bartolomé Bermejo, Rodrigo de Osona and Pedro Berruguete, whose art had a universal quality and took effect beyond the limits of the local Schools; indeed, it seems, throughout the whole Peninsula. In fact they looked like heralding a vast Renaissance—which, however, failed to eventuate, perhaps because of the basic incompatibility between a religious ideal ever growing more austere and the revival of a pagan cult of sensual beauty. Thus Spanish 16th-century art remained tinged with provincial austerity until the day when El Greco came to fructify his poetic imagination on this seemingly unfavorable soil, and dedicated the splendor of forms and the glory of color that were the birthright of his genius to the service of the unseen world and mystical expression.

But this venture was so exceptional, not to say unique, that the only effect it made on later artists (on Velazquez, especially) was an enrichment of their technical resources. It is Francisco Ribalta who may be regarded as the 'patriarch' of classical Spanish painting. Deriving his art from Valencian Mannerism, but reacting against it, he built up in conjunction with that other precursor Navarrete ('El Mudo') a sober, virile realism combined with a well-balanced 'luminism,' a technique of light effects which it would seem owed nothing to Caravaggio and ushered in the triumphs of 17th-century Spanish art.

★

Despite the havoc of the Napoleonic invasions and civil wars, Spain still possesses a vast store of works of art housed not only in her great museums and world-famous religious edifices but also in quite small towns and in family mansions. We have much pleasure in recording our gratitude to the Curators of Museums, the ecclesiastical authorities and private owners thanks to whose unfailing kindness and co-operation we have been enabled to carry out our project of illustrating Spanish art under all its aspects. One regrettable omission calls, perhaps, for mention: we have been unable to reproduce a notable, indeed epoch-making picture by Rodrigo de Osona owing to the impossibility of displacing it from the dimly lit Baptistery of the Church of San Nicolas of Valencia in which it is immoveably fixed.

We would tender thanks especially to the Marquis of Lozoya, formerly Director of Fine Arts, to the Duke of Alba by whose good offices we were given access to several private collections, to the Duchess of Lerma, to the Duke del Infantado, to Señor Antonio Zuloaga, to the Curators and staff of the Prado, the Museum of Catalan Art of Barcelona and the San Carlos Museum at Valencia; to the Keepers of the Lazaro Collection at Madrid, of the Diocesan Museums of Vich and Solsona; to the Chapter of the Cathedral of Barcelona; to the Very Reverend Mother Superior of the Convent of Pedralbes; to Señorita de Cardona, to the Reverend Father Alfonso Roig and to the Parish Priests of Tarrasa and San Nicolas of Valencia.

Since the beginning of this century vast progress has been made in the understanding and evaluation of Spanish art. Besides the great work done in this field by Tormo and Cossio, by Sanpere for Catalonia, Tramoyeres for Valencia, Gestoso for Seville; by the French *savant* Emile Bertaux, the German A. L. Mayer and the American Chandler Post (the publication of whose able and comprehensive treatise on Spanish Art is still in progress), and by that perspicacious authority on art, Eugenio d'Ors, we have now available the recent discoveries made by Fr. Sanchez Canton, Enrique Lafuente-Ferrari, Leandro de Saralegui, José Gudiol, J. Ainaud, Diego Angulo, José Camon Aznar, Gomez Moreno, Manuel Trens and Rafael Benet, whose researches have sponsored a decisive forward step in the elucidation of the chief problems of our subject. We gratefully acknowledge the assistance we have derived from the works of the above-named eminent authorities.

In most of the Provinces of Spain the local archives are now being carefully examined and collated, with the happiest results. Thus many hitherto unknown painters have come to light and the essential dates in their careers been determined. We must not conclude without a word of special commendation for the photographic archives built up during the last ten years, together with the appropriate documentation, in the Amatller Institute of Hispanic Art at Barcelona, where all the early pictures extant in Spain are systematically listed; time and again we have had recourse to this active and well-equipped cultural center.

ROMANESQUE ART IN SPAIN

★

THE ARTISTS OF TAHULL

THE SCHOOL OF THE MASTER OF PEDRET

THE ATELIERS OF URGEL

TOWARDS GOTHIC ART

ALLEGORY OF THE CRUSADES (?) (LATE ELEVENTH CENTURY).
FRESCO, APSE OF SAN QUIRCE DE PEDRET. DIOCESAN MUSEUM, SOLSONA.

ROMANESQUE ART IN SPAIN

So widespread was the flowering of Romanesque art in Europe that we are hardly justified in speaking of frontiers (which in fact did not come into effective existence until some centuries later) in this connection. Nevertheless there is no denying that this art assumed special and sometimes very different forms according to its geographical and social environment.

Thus, when we compare the Romanesque art of western and south-west France with that of Catalonia, we are at once struck by the fact that the former (seemingly the older) art has characteristics peculiar to itself and suggesting, plausibly enough, that we should see in it the offspring of some earlier art—one for instance that developed under the Carlovingians—of which nothing has survived and which originated from a complex of tendencies other than those that went to shaping the creative genius of Catalonia. In Catalan works of art, as also in the second blooming of French Romanesque (in Burgundy and Central France), Byzantine influences are far less apparent; indeed it is believed that this art was imported from Italy by Italian artists who visited or settled in Spain.

In Catalonia, also, there are traces of an older art, which sometimes suggest anterior, perhaps Roman, influences and sometimes the spontaneous effusions of an indigenous Spanish art, characterized by the naïve, almost caricatural forms we find, for instance, in the primitive frescos of the Church of San Quirce de Pedret (where, however, the delineations of animals may owe something to oriental influences). In the other early frescos, such as those at Tarrasa, the colors have faded so badly that we have little more than the bare skeletons to go on; they show leanings towards a naturalism not unlike that of such Roman painting as has survived. (It must be remembered that a highly refined Latin civilization held its ground in this part of Spain during the barbarian invasions.)

An Arab text of about the year 1000 tells of the representations made by the Spanish Christians in their churches, of the Creator, the Messiah, the Virgin and the Cross, of angels and apostles; and of their worship of these 'images'. This shows that at this date a Romanesque art was in existence, and a symbolic ritual had already formed around it, though judging by the remains at Tarrasa, we gather that what was chiefly aimed at was the group significance of the figures. On the other hand, the archaic frescos at San Quirce de Pedret, with their gauche, rather childish representations of themes probably stemming from contemporary events (in this case, some think, the preaching of a crusade), have touches of realistic detail which, much simplified as they are, make good by their enhanced emotive power.

It would seem, therefore, that the flowering of Romanesque which took place at the beginning of the 11th century was due, not to an evolution of these early archaic schools, but to contacts with artists who came (or returned) to Spain from Italy, perhaps by way of the South of France. These artists had encountered in Italy the art tendencies which, fanning out from their starting-point, Mount Athos, spread through Dalmatia, Venetia, Aemilia and Sicily and left their mark on the great basilicas adorned with mosaics and on a certain early type of fresco, which as yet has not been adequately studied.

Catalan painting reached perfection with remarkable suddenness, finding appropriate forms and the majesty distinctive of it almost from the start. These early and exemplary achievements served as points of departure for various local schools, in which, however, autochthonous forms steadily bulked larger; thus in these schools this art tended gradually to degenerate, though certain individualist qualities came to the fore, pointing the way to new developments.

To begin with, the drawing was taken from a repertory of stereotyped pictorial formulae permitting a limited number of gestures and facial expressions readily understandable by the spectator, and ensuring a simple, dignified rendering of themes. However, as time went on, details of execution tended to become more realistic and to approximate to the painters' observation. Likewise as regards the colors the artists began by keeping to a strictly defined convention in which cool or warm tones corresponded to the nature of the figure in question or evoked a specific ambiance. Meager at first and limited to 'earthy' colors, yellow ochres, reds, green and bistres, they were soon enriched by blendings and gradations from one hue to another in the transitional passages. Then carmines, blues and vermilions made their appearance and the artists, over-riding the conventional symbolism attaching to these colors, used them for more frankly representational ends.

The Catalan artists employed the usual direct fresco process, but supplemented it with retouchings. The true *buonfresco* process was used only for the ground colors; the drawing, modeling, and expressive touches were put on later, upon a very thin coat of wet plaster superimposed on the wall surface. Thanks to this procedure, these after-touches have held fairly well and the whole composition usually gives an impression of over-all technical unity.

Hardly anything is known about the artists responsible for the great Romanesque painting of Catalonia. Happily their works, after a long period of oblivion, have been rescued in the nick of time. Now that they are housed in the museums of Barcelona, Gerona, Solsona and even in the Prado, they have been studied closely by the experts who installed and restored them, and it has been possible to make much progress in appraising them aesthetically and critically. The research-work of Gudiol and Ainaud, in particular, has borne good fruit and even at this early stage the masters to whom the most striking of these frescos are to be ascribed can be identified beyond all doubt.

Gudiol has drawn attention to four such master-artists, pioneers and founders of schools, whose influence can be traced in many of the minor works. We may begin by a study of the Masters of Tahull and Maderuelo, whose works can be identified with some precision; next we shall consider the artist group centering on the Master of Pedret, and then the ateliers of Urgel, in which the work of the leader of each school is indistinguishable from that of his disciples.

A case apart is the Master of Bohi whose only known work is the fresco in the Church of San Juan at Bohi (Province of Lerida) and who cuts the figure of a precursor in the sense

THE MASTER OF BOHI. BEAST OF THE APOCALYPSE (EARLY TWELFTH CENTURY).
FRESCO, NAVE OF SAN JUAN DE BOHI. MUSEUM OF CATALAN ART, BARCELONA.

THE MASTER OF THE LAST JUDGMENT. DAVID VICTORIOUS (EARLY TWELFTH CENTURY).
FRESCO, NAVE OF SANTA MARIA DE TAHULL. MUSEUM OF CATALAN ART, BARCELONA.

that his work diverges with some boldness from the Byzantine canon. Probably he stands
for a local style of art (in which the representation of animals played a large part), but was
endowed with exceptional talent. Here the tall, gracefully elongated figures wear the
costumes of the period, tunics and broad trousers reminiscent of Asia Minor—which may
be explained by the fact that the East Coast of Spain had been frequented by Syrian traders

long before the Arab invasions. Already we have here that background of horizontal stripes of color which figures so often in the Romanesque art of Catalonia (as in France, at Brinay) and which at once serves to balance the vertical stance of the figures and to give them relief and solidity. The vigorous drawing seems to owe more to direct personal observation than to imitation of any accepted model. Unique of its kind, indeed a masterpiece, this work may be regarded as the most perfect specimen of the art of those few local schools which—before disappearing for ever under the impact of technically superior procedures imported from abroad—lit on similar techniques and employed them to excellent effect. We find echoes of this personal accent and coloristic vehemence in the works of some lesser masters (to whom reference will be made), such as the Master of the Last Judgment, and these men are generally held to be representative of indigenous traditions as against the artists from abroad who founded schools in Spain.

THE ARTISTS OF TAHULL

The Master of Tahull stands out beyond all question as the leading figure of Catalan Romanesque; indeed this village of the Pyrenees may be regarded as a shrine of Romanesque art, for it was here that, in 1123, were built and consecrated two famous churches which rank amongst its most notable memorials. At San Clemente the Master of Tahull worked on the chief decorations, and at Santa Maria the Master of Maderuelo; while the lower portions of both edifices contain hardly less interesting decorations by the Master of the Last Judgment. In the architecture of both churches there are markedly Italian characteristics—which confirm the theory that a group of visiting Italian architects took part in their building—and they served as models for neighboring churches subsequently built at Erill, Dourro and elsewhere. The two churches were consecrated by that learned prelate Bishop Ramondus to whose enterprise their erection was probably due. Tahull belonged to the Baron of Erill, vassal of the Count of Pallars-Jussa, a member of the Court of Alfonso the Battler, King of Aragon and conqueror of the Moors at Tudela and Cutanda, who liberated Saragossa, henceforth the real center of the Aragonese dominion. Ramondus was his almoner. Alfonso married Urraca, heiress of the Kingdom of Castile. Thus it is natural enough that we should find the works and the influence of the two Masters who worked at Tahull both in the regions under the sway of Aragon and in the dependencies of Old Castile which were temporarily united with them.

The Master of Tahull put into practice the canons of traditional Byzantine art in, to all intents and purposes, their purest state; thus he is generally thought to have come from abroad, already in full possession of his technique. For, quite obviously, there is nothing tentative about this art, it is highly accomplished and handled with consummate ease. True, each figure stands for a symbol, but besides this—and it is why this artist strikes us as a great master—we find a faculty of expressing truly human values, all the more effective for the restraint with which they are expressed. The perfect rhythm of the composition implements the nuances and the delicate rendering of details, each of which is given an individual significance; thus the face, hand and feet of the Pantocrator, and the hand of God the Father, are vibrant with life. Each of the figures in the lower part of the composition—the Virgin, for example—tells out in turn and the exaggerations in these forms —for instance the width of the nostrils and the curves of the mouth—are clearly intentional and not due to inexpertness. The quality and skilful modulations of the colors and the transitional passages speak for an artist in full possession of his craft. It seems that immediately after finishing the apse of San Clemente and painting the keystone of the vault, on which are shown the Hand of God and the Lamb with Seven Eyes of the Apocalypse, the Master of Tahull left this village and started work on the decoration of the old cathedral of Roda de Isbena (Province of Huesca). Little of this work has survived, but the painter's influence is manifest in the decorations of many churches in the neighborhood.

THE MASTER OF TAHULL. CHRIST PANTOCRATOR (EARLY TWELFTH CENTURY).
FRESCO, APSE OF SAN CLEMENTE DE TAHULL. MUSEUM OF CATALAN ART, BARCELONA.

Another painter, probably an associate of the Master in question and belonging to the same school, was employed on the apse of the second church at Tahull. While the proportions of his work are less grandiose and there is less inventiveness in the treatment of traditional themes, he displays much vigor, especially in the forthright drawing of the faces and, though the content of his decorations is inferior, he imparts expressiveness to them

THE MASTER OF TAHULL. THE HAND OF GOD (EARLY TWELFTH CENTURY).
FRESCO, TRIUMPHAL ARCH OF SAN CLEMENTE DE TAHULL. MUSEUM OF CATALAN ART, BARCELONA.

by his highly skilful draftsmanship. There are grounds for believing that this second Master was bidden to Castile and made the frescos at Maderuelo (Province of Segovia) —hence the name 'The Master of Maderuelo' by which he is generally known—and also some of the decorations of the famous Hermitage of San Baudelio at Berlanga (Province of Soria). Particularly noteworthy in the Maderuelo frescos (now in the Prado) are their balanced structure and fine proportions; in fact this master of Catalan Romanesque

THE MASTER OF TAHULL. LAZARUS THE BEGGAR (EARLY TWELFTH CENTURY).
FRESCO, TRIUMPHAL ARCH OF SAN CLEMENTE DE TAHULL. MUSEUM OF CATALAN ART, BARCELONA.

might be styled its classicist *par excellence*. At Berlanga, where he decorated the arches and vaults with biblical scenes, his work must have suffered to some extent by the presence just below it of some very striking decorations (whether earlier or later in date it is impossible to say) in which the artist, probably of Moorish origin, depicted hunting scenes, including such exotic animals as elephants and camels. These decorations most brilliantly combine the suggestion of rapid movement with a strict economy of line.

The painting of the side walls of the two churches at Tahull was assigned to a third artist and, especially in the Church of Santa Maria, his work is of a very high order. He had more freedom in his choice of subjects than the painters of the vaults, who were obliged to portray Christ or the Madonna surrounded by apostles or evangelists, and he had larger surfaces to work on. Taking his themes from the Bible and notably the Apocalypse, he handled them in an original manner and often with much boldness. His depiction of Hell has earned him his appellation, "The Master of the Last Judgment." He seems to find a rather morbid delectation in displaying souls or, rather, bodies suffering the torments of the damned, the tormentors being devils and snakes which are greedily devouring the victims' heads and limbs. On the epistle-side of the altar (where the painting is in better condition) is a sequence of skilfully arranged scenes amongst which figure a boat with an angel and a passenger on board, Herod and the Magi, Zacharias, a curious white bull and the Virgin framed in an aureole. Last but not least—it originally figured in a side nave—is one of the most remarkable creations of Catalan Romanesque art: a synthetic rendering of the David and Goliath story. Here the artist was evidently given a free hand, the stylization is not governed by any ritual significance or convention but solely by the natural sequence of the events depicted. Thus the hand thrust forth from the giant's coat of mail is elongated in such a way as to suggest both a hand and an arm, and its gesture might be one of homage or entreaty. The painter has dressed his characters in the costumes of the age; Goliath is wearing the heavy gear of the foot-soldier, with lance and buckler, while David has a short tunic and conical headdress. The bird in the background seems oddly rigid, like a heraldic figure, but there is nothing of this sort in the animals painted above the combatants or in the drawing of the bull (in the adjoining panel) whose leg swings forward with a supple movement like that of the lamb in the Maderuelo composition. The colors employed by this painter, believed to have been a Catalan, differ from those of the two masters previously commented on; like those of the Master of Bohi, they are limited in range, ochre and carmine predominating, but richly charged with pigment. The decorative elements, too, have a highly effective simplicity, while the movement of the transverse bands permeates the whole composition. The figures do not so much stand out as come to life and smoothly glide across a broadly decorated backcloth. What we have here is not that uniform background, whether bright or shadowy—of open sky or darkness—which is found in so many Byzantine mosaics and in the Romanesque art of western France and strikes a contrast with the action in the foreground; the effect is much more like that of tapestry, whose technique is prefigured in the handling of drapery.

The exceptional importance of the Tahull group of paintings is emphasized by the connection that has been traced between certain aspects of these works and the subsequent development of Romanesque painting throughout the whole of northern Spain. A problem of particular interest, since it presupposes the parallel and simultaneous emergence of those two initial art forms—fresco painting on walls and the altar decorations which led up to the retable—is that of determining the exact relationship between the work of the Master of Tahull himself and the painting on the Ribas baldachin, which can justly be regarded as at once the most striking and probably the earliest example of Catalan painting on wood. Only a fragment of this baldachin survives (depicting Christ Pantocrator surrounded by angels). When we compare this with, on the one hand, the apse of San Clemente of Tahull (Christ with the Evangelists) and, on the other, the frontal of Seo de Urgel (Christ with the Apostles) we see at once that the Ribas baldachin stands precisely midway between the two last-named works. Its technique is still very near that of the fresco; the colors are soft, as though diluted in water, and there are subtle transitions in the azure blues. The drawing, especially in the looks imparted to the faces, is full of human understanding and delicate sentiment. While we can almost certainly identify the maker of the frontals at Urgel and at Hix with the painter of the frescos in the Church of Seo de Urgel, all we can say about the painter of the Ribas frontal is that he comes very near the Master of Tahull, more in virtue of his high technical proficiency and the human appeal of his art than because of any specific resemblances of detail.

ST JOHN THE EVANGELIST (MIDDLE OF TWELFTH CENTURY).
FRESCO, CHURCH OF ARGOLELL. MUSEUM OF CATALAN ART, BARCELONA.

THE SCHOOL OF THE MASTER OF PEDRET

As against the two great masters of Tahull who stand for Byzantine orthodoxy and whose personalities are so conspicuous that the time seems near when, as a result of patient research-work, we shall know something about the men themselves—as against these two outstanding artists, two other men, the Master of Pedret and the Master of Urgel, stand for two varieties of a more specifically indigenous art. We have an impression of two large schools flourishing side by side, well organized and grouping together a great number of artists of various descriptions—fresco-painters, painters on wood and sculptors—whose leading figures we are still attempting to segregate from the rank-and-file. Thus in this field ascriptions are less positive, the works themselves less coherent, and conclusions harder to come by. The Master of Pedret, who made in the famous Mozarabic Church of San Quirce the decorations which now are housed in the museums of Solsona and Barcelona, was undoubtedly one of the most original of all Catalan artists. No less remarkable than his gift for imparting to high religious subjects the simple charm of scenes of everyday life and to every face a look of gentle yet alert interest, is the loving care he bestows on details, on flowers and decorative accessories (which he treats in the manner of still lifes), the lifelikeness of his rendering of animals in movement (for example the horses of the Apocalypse), and the boldness with which he adds a touch of humor here and there (e.g. the knight bestriding a huge bird). Indeed we may see in the Master of Pedret one of the first artists to reveal the inner life pervading everything on earth, and his scenes often remind us of the detailed yet strangely clairvoyant imagery characteristic of Coptic art.

Though they have some almost too obvious resemblances (notably in the drawing) to the work of the Master of Pedret, I question if that wonderful cupola of Santa Maria de Esterri at Aneu and the decorations of San Pedro at Burgal should be ascribed to him. There is no doubt that a whole school drew inspiration from the Master of Pedret, but the peculiar merit of his achievement lay precisely in his unfailing gift for making a wholly original work out of hackneyed themes. Thus the hall-mark of the master should be looked for not in the outward trappings but in the content of the picture. The painter of Santa Maria de Esterri seems to me to have a sort of distinction, not to say detachment, and a mastery of his subject-matter peculiar to himself. The artist of Burgal, on the other hand, with his severe, highly competent formalism, lacks warmth, and I would assign him to a later period. Belonging certainly to the same group and holding a high place in it were two other artists, who worked at the Castle of Orcau and in the small near-by country church respectively. Their saints (whose bodies are only slightly elongated), while full of dignity, are real people; their colors, though the range is small, carry conviction, and they handle their composition more broadly, making it dovetail into a natural setting, a briefly indicated landscape, with an expanse of grass and flowers. Nor must we fail to mention the painter of San Pedro de Sorpe who, awkward as is his execution, strikes a note of real tenderness in his *Virgin Annunciate*. On the whole, the works of this cycle show much progress in the handling of color; no longer dictated solely by a rigid, age-old symbolism, it is brought into ever closer touch with natural appearances.

This art, which arose in the Valley of the Noguera Pallaresa, extending from the Val d'Aran in the Province of Lerida to the neighborhood of Berga in the Province of Barcelona, vouches for a highly interesting attempt to impart an individual accent to the treatment of conventional themes. In all these works the artist makes us aware of his personal responses, the emotions he feels when confronting one of the great religious mysteries. In the fact that, though the general lay-out admitted of so little variation, the artist has succeeded in imparting so distinctive an atmosphere to each of his works, we have perhaps the earliest example of that process of transmutation of the subject in the artist's mind—the alchemy of art—which lies at the base of western painting. And what is so remarkable, and demonstrates the creative originality of this early Catalan school, is that this holds good not only for one or two but for a whole group of painters.

THE MASTER OF PEDRET. ABEL OFFERING FLOWERS TO THE LORD (MIDDLE OF TWELFTH CENTURY).
FRESCO, CENTRAL NAVE OF SAN QUIRCE DE PEDRET. DIOCESAN MUSEUM, SOLSONA.

THE ATELIERS OF URGEL

The fourth group operated further north, in the heart of the Pyrenees, around the ancient diocesan center of Urgel. The work of these artists covered a large field: polychrome sculpture, frescos, mural decoration and painting on wood for the ornamental panels in front of altars known as 'frontals' and the baldachins—which preceded the retable *(retrotabulum)*, the painted screen or reredos *behind* the altar. (It was this region that sponsored, a century later, the first known retable, a rudimentary one, in St Martin's Church at Angustrina near Bourg-Madame on the Spanish frontier of France.) Hence the strongly decorative trend of this school, its tendency to load the picture with embossed and gilded ornaments. The motifs of these decorations were not merely geometrical but often taken from the vegetable kingdom, and there were persistent attempts to import effects of goldsmiths' work and sculpture into painting, use being made of the techniques of veneering and *pastillage* (the application of previously modeled ornamental details, as on the cornices of ceilings). Many artists and craftsmen were employed in the production of these retables whose influence was lasting, making itself felt even in the Gothic painting of the School of Barcelona.

Some regard the painter who decorated the cupola of San Pedro's church, in the shadow of the Cathedral, as having been the leading figure of the School of Urgel. But was it not rather the artist responsible for those two masterpieces of painting on wood: the frontals of Hix and Urgel? For, though he had only a relatively small area to work on, he achieved in each case the majesty and monumental proportions of the Pantocrator of San Clemente de Tahull. Quite possibly the frescos and paintings at Urgel were also by his hand; the figures and especially the garments with their thickly blocked-in folds are treated in a very similar manner. In the Urgel frontal, as in the frescos of the apse, we find decorative motifs from the vegetable kingdom (these are, however, more elaborately developed in the frescos). The reason why the frontals have a more immediate emotive appeal is probably that the technique

CHRIST PANTOCRATOR AND APOSTLES (EARLY TWELFTH CENTURY).
FRONTAL OF SEO DE URGEL. MUSEUM OF CATALAN ART, BARCELONA.

CHRIST PANTOCRATOR AND ANGELS (EARLY TWELFTH CENTURY).
BALDACHIN OF RIBAS. MUSEUM OF VICH.

of such painting lent itself to effects of greater intensity. For, generally speaking, the fresco technique, which involves dilution of the pigment in water and its application to a moist ground of mixed lime and sand (or in a good many cases to an already existing, but moistened plaster wall) makes for a certain attenuation of the colors. Only a few 'folk' or archaic works (like those of Bohi and those by the Master of the Last Judgment) retain a certain forcefulness. In the frontals, however, where the pigment, mixed with the contents of an egg, has been applied in thick layers on a wooden ground, dressed probably with a thin coat of resin, the colors (at once bolder and more varied than in the frescos) are far more vivid, while the figures, bound with black contour-lines, tell out strongly against the background.

It is no easy matter assigning a date to these frontals. The archaic touches and clumsiness we find in some of them—though actually the technique of such painting was simpler and more widely practised than that of the fresco—have led many to think that they preceded the frescos and to assign them to the beginning of the 12th century or even the end of the 11th (like the famous Montgrony frontal in the Vich Museum). I am inclined to share the views of Gudiol, who sees no good ground for this chronology. It seems far likelier that after the first dramatic impact of Byzantine art in the early 12th century, the artists of the Urgel group (whose craftsmanship was of the highest order) transposed, so to speak, these pictures from the wall on to the wooden panels of the altar, or from the vault on to the wooden canopy of the baldachin, which thus acted as a substitute for it. If this be so, the oldest of these frontals would date from the mid-twelfth century, and be those representing Christ Pantocrator and the Apostles, and then the Virgin in Glory. It was only later and by slow degrees that the saints—the patron saints of the various churches, to begin with—made their appearance; though obviously the smaller dimensions of the frontal and its relative cheapness favored the presentation of these minor religious subjects. Then anecdotal elements began to work their way into the picture, which now included picturesque or striking details taken from everyday life, and became a sort of illustrated Golden Legend. Thus this form of art tended gradually to lose its vigor and to fritter itself away on private acts of devotion and local rites: subjects which even the most rustic and least skilful artists made bold to handle. Nevertheless, this homelier art brought compensations, for it opened the artist's eyes on the real world and quickened his sense of wonder.

ST MARTIN AND THE BEGGAR (EARLY TWELFTH CENTURY).
FRONTAL OF HIX, DETAIL. MUSEUM OF CATALAN ART, BARCELONA.

24

ST MARTIN ON HORSEBACK CUTTING HIS MANTLE (MIDDLE OF TWELFTH CENTURY).
FRONTAL OF MONTGRONY, DETAIL. MUSEUM OF VICH.

So it was that, now that the Byzantine iconography had been transposed on to wood, the School of Urgel came to include a host of 'little masters' who, though inexpert, were keenly observant and illustrated better than the fresco-painters the life of the world around them. The popular character this art rapidly assumed may be one of the reasons why it kept so happily immune from the aridity and lack of vitality found in the iconography of the East.

The School of Urgel demonstrates the intimate connection between the mural art of the time and painting on wood, not only in the rustic paintings on the walls and crosses of the churches of Andorra, but also in the work of those fine artists who migrated to Vich and Ripoll—which likewise became great centers of painting on wood. Thus one of the most interesting exhibits in the Museum of Vich, the frontal of Espinelvas, has been positively identified—by reason of the attitudes of the figures and details of the costumes—as the work of the same artist as the painter of the apse of Santa Maria de Tarrasa, north of Barcelona, where, under a 'Christ in Majesty,' is depicted an incident of contemporary history, the murder of Thomas Becket, Archbishop of Canterbury. This took place in 1170, Becket was canonized three years later and the cult of the martyr saint spread rapidly through western Christendom, a chapel being dedicated to him in Toledo Cathedral in 1174, and an altar in the Barcelona Cathedral in 1196. Thus we can safely ascribe to the close of the 12th century the frontal mentioned above, a relatively unambitious work of small dimensions, but having a vivacity and a direct appeal more characteristic of painting on wood than of traditional fresco art on the grand scale.

However, after its escape from the rigidity of the Byzantine procedures, Catalan Romanesque art succeeded in solving, without extraneous aid, one of its basic stylistic

THE MASTER OF ESPINELVAS. ENTRY OF CHRIST INTO JERUSALEM (CA. 1187). FRONTAL OF ESPINELVAS, DETAIL. MUSEUM OF VICH.

THE MASTER OF ESPINELVAS. MARTYRDOM OF ST THOMAS BECKET, DETAIL (CA. 1190).
FRESCO, LATERAL APSE OF SANTA MARIA DE TARRASA.

THE MASTER OF LLUSSANES. ANGEL MUSICIANS (EARLY THIRTEENTH CENTURY).
FRESCO, VAULT OF THE TOMB OF SAN PABLO DE CASSERRES. DIOCESAN MUSEUM, SOLSONA.

problems. Already in the great frontals emanating from the ateliers of Urgel we find a transformation of the traditional stylizations being effected, by means of the drawing alone. One of the most striking examples is the frontal of Montgrony. In it we see the painter multiplying the lines of his calligraphy, twisting and bending them to his will; for instance, he both doubles the line of the eyebrow and gives it a steep downward curve so as to stress the humble entreaty of the poor man who is begging St Martin to give him half his cloak —a skilful touch of symbolism that would have delighted Seurat. Another no less interesting section of the same frontal shows a blind man standing before the saint; in this case the closed eye is represented by a single line and the impression of blindness is ingeniously emphasized by the three parallel, undulating lines inscribed above it. Here we have a touch of original creative talent; dissatisfied with the signs placed at his disposal by tradition or previous experience, the artist has invented a stenography of his own to implement the emotive effect he has in mind.

For—and this is a point we do well to bear in mind—the Romanesque artist, even when he felt himself free to follow his own bent, was possessed by an urge to synthesis.

THE MASTER OF LLUSSANES. THE ANNUNCIATION (EARLY THIRTEENTH CENTURY).
FRONTAL OF LLUSSA, DETAIL. MUSEUM OF VICH.

ATELIER OF LERIDA. LIFE OF ST CLEMENT (THIRTEENTH CENTURY).
FRONTAL OF TAHULL. MUSEUM OF CATALAN ART, BARCELONA.

This is particularly noticeable at the beginning of the 12th century when Byzantine influence was waning; a new vocabulary was being compiled, differing from its predecessor by the fact that it stemmed directly from observation of the real world, yet, nevertheless, comprising a wealth of simplifications and 'idioms' nowise inferior to those of Byzantine art. Thus, even in this early age, an art specifically Catalan had come into the world. Noteworthy illustrations of it are to be found in the work of the Master of Llussanes, both in the frescos of the tomb of San Pablo de Casserres and in the frontal of *The Life of the Virgin* (Museum of Vich) in which each scene—e.g. *The Annunciation* and *The Flight into Egypt*—forms an organic whole, all the lines combining in a perfect harmony. At the Church of Santa Maria de Tarrasa, there is a fresco, *The Dormition of the Virgin*, dating from about the same period, in which the drawing is reduced to contour-lines, volumes being suggested only by inflexions of these contour-lines or accents placed upon them, while the colors have become irrelevant; with the result that the composition resolves itself into an almost abstract arrangement of surface patterns.

The Romanesque art of Catalonia and Aragon reached its full flowering in a little less than a century. It continued to flourish for an approximately equal period, under more anecdotal and less cumbrous forms, in the secular as well as the religious domain. Actually only a very few large-scale decorations of the walls of churches were made during the 13th century—with the notable exception of the Chapter House of the Monastery of Sigena, in whose sumptuous ornamentation the influence of the near-by Moors is unmistakable, the woodwork, ceiling and panelling being in the Mozarabic style. But the most interesting decorative work of the period is to be seen on its tombs; on the walls of palaces (e.g. the warrior groups figuring on the walls of the Old Royal Palace of Barcelona, and the battle-scenes at the Castle of Alcañiz); and, lastly, on the walls of certain private houses (vestiges of a very striking mural decoration have been discovered in a house at Barcelona).

TOWARDS GOTHIC ART

In dealing with this secular pre-Gothic art we come up against problems relating in a general way to the life of Spain as a whole during this period, when the populations of different regions were growing aware of their racial kinship. We have seen that during the 12th century the only decorative works produced in Castile can be ascribed unquestionably to the Master of Maderuelo, who came there from the East. But there also existed, towards the close of the same century, another great ensemble of works of art, and a very striking one, at the royal city of Leon, Pantheon of the Catholic Kings. The art of this school is quite exceptional (for its time and place); such, indeed, is the elegance of its decorations, the rich diversity of its animal forms and the delicate charm of its figures that it has often been ascribed to some master-artist coming from western France. (It is known that French artists and sculptors were to be found all along the pilgrims' route to Compostella throughout the High Middle Ages.) Whereas in Catalonia and Aragon the large-scale works are accompanied by a host of minor ones—suggesting that a number of artists pooled their knowledge and discoveries—nothing of this sort took place in western Spain. It was not until the end of the 13th century that there arose in Castile, Leon and Galicia a local art, still rather crude and smacking of the soil, to compete with the work being done by the artists of the eastern provinces. Little studied and all but unknown as are these western schools, they produced some outstanding works, such as the frescos made (and signed) by Andrés Sanchez of Segovia in the chapel of the Old Cathedral of Salamanca. (Mayer believes that the date 1262 written on this work is spurious, its real date being round about 1300.)

The very lay-out of this chapel, the decoration representing a Gothic edifice in which the sacred figures are inset, as if in windows (noteworthy being a superb St Martin), and the imaginative yet homely treatment of religious themes—much as they were to be treated some years later by the Flemish Primitives—all alike point to a great change impending in the western world.

In fact the 13th century witnessed the transition from the monastic régime to the secular. Hitherto the religious Orders (of Cluny, then Citeaux) had guided the great ventures of Romanesque art, given them their oecumenical accent, supplied them with a coherent program and a set technique and by these means created a sort of universal language. But from now on the Orders were no longer arbiters of the economic and social evolution of western Christendom. The growth of cities and townships was now conditioned by the local trades and handicrafts; kingdoms were consolidated and royal courts grew wealthy.

THE LAST SUPPER (LATE THIRTEENTH CENTURY).
FRONTAL OF SURIGUEROLA, DETAIL. MUSEUM OF CATALAN ART, BARCELONA.

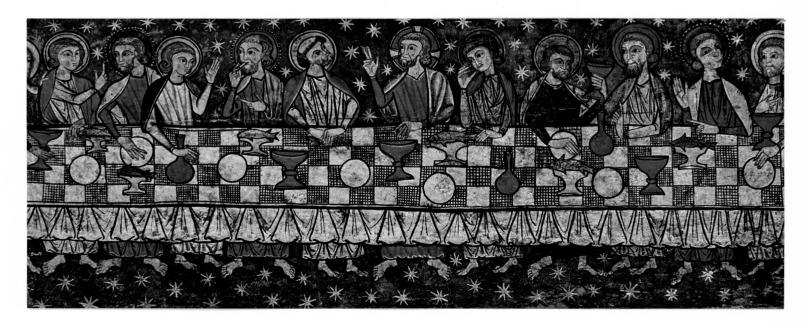

The changes that came over architecture affected the decorative arts. The church was no longer a meditative sort of place bathed in a 'dim, religious light'; now great domes soared heavenwards, riddled by shafts of sunlight, and below them huge crowds joined in prayer and pious exultation. Thus there was no longer any question of painting the walls, which, on the contrary, were opened up to let the daylight in, and a new art came to the fore, all translucency and glowing color: that of the stained-glass window. Painting now played a less spectacular, though still important part; in the chapels the frontal was supplanted by the retable, which soon grew to a considerable size, while its illustrative and narrative possibilities were exploited all the more assiduously because, in Spain, the art of stained glass was never carried to the same pitch as in France.

It seems quite likely that some panels painted at the close of the 13th century were moved up from below the altar to a place above it—which entailed certain changes in perspective and composition. Mayer thinks that the frontal at Avia, in which the central figure is no longer enclosed in an oval and the bottom of the composition suggests that it was meant to rest on another mass, may have been intended to be treated in this manner. In this work the joint influence of the miniature and French stained glass is evident and has led to drastic changes in the lay-out. During this period the frontals were no longer dominated by a single, all-pervading rhythm; the narration was divided into equal parts and the central figure tended to disappear. The treatment of the whole is far more diversified, narrative scenes being elongated and intersected by vertical figures. In one of the most characteristic of these works, the frontal of the Master of Suriguerola, the dissymmetry is pronounced, the length-wise presentation of the Last Supper being contrasted with a sort of checkerboard of figures, and each element of the pattern treated independently.

This isolation of each unit ended up by being complete; thus each panel of the tomb of Sancho Saiz de Carillo (originally at Mahamud in the Province of Burgos) deals with a separate scene—though the work as a whole is a combination of these scenes, which complement each other and form a sequence. Of the six panels two depict escutcheons and the four others groups of men and women taking part in a funeral procession. The big woollen mantles dyed black, brown and yellow are certainly faithful reproductions of the garments of the time. What, however, strikes us most is the dramatic vigor of the attitudes and the way in which the bands of color traversing, horizontally or diagonally, the verticals of the bodies no longer ribbon the background (as in the early murals), but are supplied by the materials of the garments.

Thus a sort of easel-painting replaced the mural; its function was still for the most part religious, but it drew its inspiration more and more from real life. These works were commissioned by local civic authorities, by the powerful merchant guilds of Barcelona, by rich donors, monarchs, ministers of the Crown, enlightened noblemen and pious individuals, and, naturally enough, the tastes of these patrons made themselves felt in the works they ordered and in which they made a point of figuring. During this period a painting was commonly regarded as an object of commerce, on a par with jewellery; in fact everything made by a skilled artist or craftsman was on the same footing. At Barcelona the various guilds of craftsmen formed a class of citizens uniformly described as 'artists.' What now was asked of the work of art was that it should be easy to carry about, to barter or to sell, and a steady traffic in works of art developed between the provinces of Spain. The 'schools' were no longer restricted to organized and strictly disciplined groups, but provided workshops in which all the workers had equal rights and the individual could exercise his talents to the best advantage and follow his own bent. The prosperity of France in the 13th and at the beginning of the 14th century affected Spain simultaneously, or with only a slight time-lag, and the arts of stained glass, the miniature and tapestry had parallel developments on both sides of the Pyrenees. Tuscan painting, then in its heyday, also made its influence felt even in the remotest regions of the Peninsula. And when, in the 15th century, the hegemony of art passed into the hands of the wealthy townships of Flanders and Burgundy, the 'new' technique of painting in oils rapidly made its way into every part of Andalusia.

FUNERAL PROCESSIONS (LATE THIRTEENTH CENTURY). TOMB OF SANCHO SAIZ DE CARILLO, MAHAMUD.
MUSEUM OF CATALAN ART, BARCELONA.

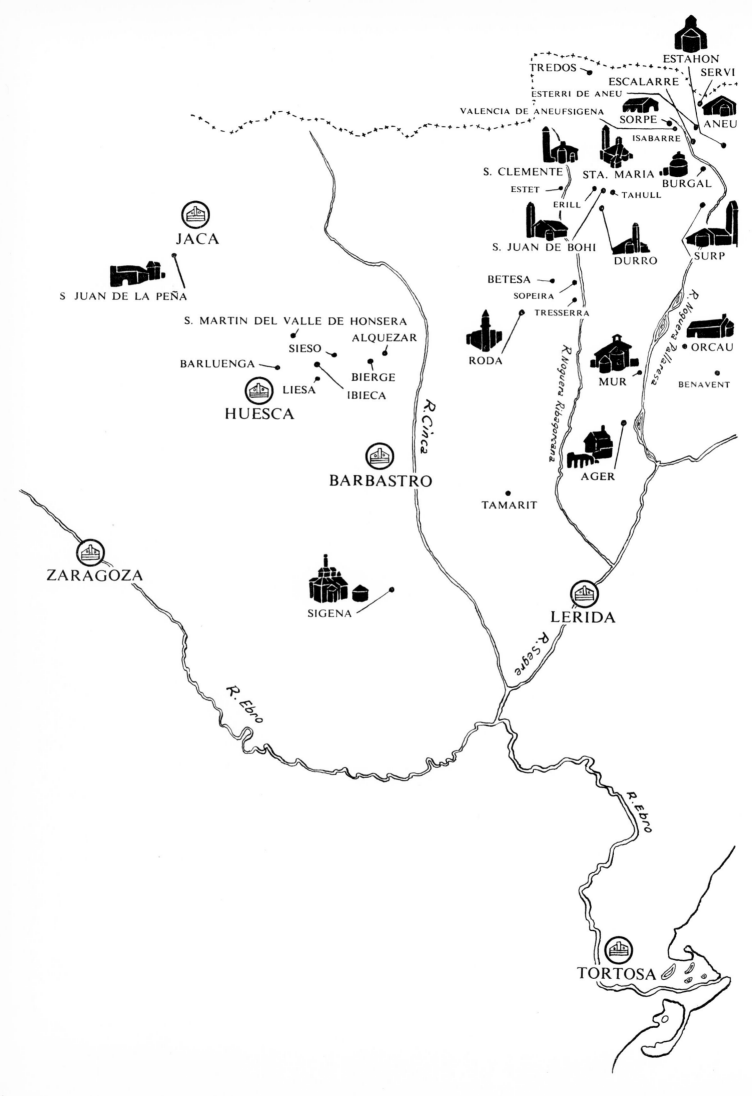

ESTAHON

TREDOS

ESCALARRE

SERVI

ESTERRI DE ANEU

VALENCIA DE ANEUFSIGENA

SORPE

ANEU

ISABARRE

S. CLEMENTE

STA. MARIA

BURGAL

ESTET

TAHULL

ERILL

S. JUAN DE BOHI

DURRO

SURP

BETESA

SOPEIRA

TRESSERRA

JACA

RODA

R. Noguera Pallaresa

R. Noguera Ribagorzana

ORCAU

S JUAN DE LA PEÑA

MUR

BENAVENT

S. MARTIN DEL VALLE DE HONSERA

ALQUEZAR

SIESO

BARLUENGA

BIERGE

LIESA

IBIECA

HUESCA

AGER

BARBASTRO

TAMARIT

R. Cinca

ZARAGOZA

SIGENA

LERIDA

R. Segre

R. Ebro

R. Ebro

TORTOSA

34

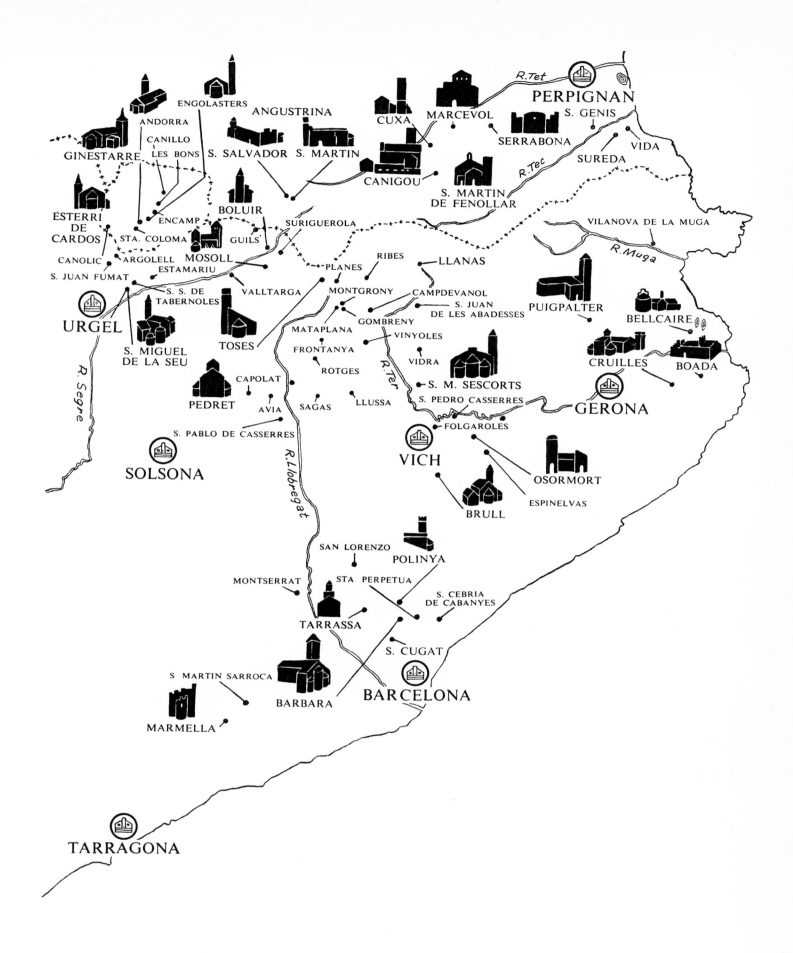

MAP OF THE ROMANESQUE SANCTUARIES IN CATALONIA AND ARAGON
(MAP DRAWN UP BY THE MUSEUM OF CATALAN ART, BARCELONA)

THE PRIMITIVES

★

FERRER BASSA

CATALAN PAINTING

THE SCHOOL OF VALENCIA

HUGUET AND THE LAST PHASE OF THE CATALAN SCHOOL

THE ADVENT OF NORTHERN TECHNIQUES

BERMEJO AND RODRIGO DE OSONA

FERRER BASSA (?-1348). PENTECOST (1345-1346).
CONVENT OF PEDRALBES.

FERRER BASSA (?-1348). THE NATIVITY (1345-1346). CONVENT OF PEDRALBES.

THE PRIMITIVES

WE are too apt to assume that, during the Middle Ages and the Renaissance, only Italy and the Low Countries gave birth to art of international significance and that the whole future of European art was conditioned by the evolution of their schools. This is a misconception, particularly where Spain is concerned; as early as the beginning of the 14th century several extremely active art centers, with many quite original productions to their credit, flourished in the Peninsula. The fact that over a thousand painters are known to have been working at this time says much for the fertility of Primitive Spanish art. Amongst this number certain great artists stand out, who succeed, complement and throw light on each other (even when their paths diverge). Naturally Spanish works often show signs of Italian, Flemish and even German and French influences, but we should be entirely wrong in thinking that these were decisive or even preponderant. Actually Catalan and Valencian painting sponsored an art which, once it is better known (and we hope the illustrations in this book will contribute to that end), may well be judged worthy to rank beside the greatest non-Spanish schools.

FERRER BASSA

Some great 12th-century works of art have come down to us. But though records of the period cite the names of a vast number of painters who flourished during the 13th century—at the close of which the transition from works of huge dimensions to the new art of the altarpieces had been accomplished—no work by any of them is extant. This much, however, can be gathered from the records: that already an intense artistic activity reigned in Catalonia. Thus there is mention of workshop-studios and whole families of artists such as the Emfos and the Crous. Under these circumstances it is difficult to know exactly when and how the first Italian influences took effect and what soil was first to receive their fertilizing contact. Certainly they count for little in the work of Ferrer Bassa, a painter of great originality, standing outside the main stream of Spanish art. Unfortunately, though his career seems to have covered approximately the same period as those of Simone Martini and the brothers Lorenzetti (he died in 1348 and is believed to have been born in or about 1285), the only works we have by him belong to the closing years of his life. These are the murals he painted for the chapel of the Convent of Pedralbes, the contract for which was signed in 1343. The artist started work on them at Easter, 1345, and finished them on November 23, 1346. This work, the artist's swan-song, is of outstanding interest both for the scale on which it was conceived and for its excellent state of preservation, and looking at it we regret the more keenly that all this artist's other paintings have disappeared.

Ferrer Bassa was a leading figure of his time; Court Painter to Pedro IV, King of Aragon, he was a *persona grata* at the Court and entrusted with important diplomatic missions. Records are extant of various commissions he received. Thus we learn of his supplying altarpieces for the chapel of the Palace of Lerida in 1316; in 1324 he made paintings in two chapels at Sitges; in 1332 and in 1342 two altarpieces for the altars of the Virgin and St Stephen at Saragossa; an altarpiece illustrating the Story of the Holy Cross for the chapel of the Castle of Perpignan; another for the Royal Palace at Barcelona. Not a trace of any of these paintings survives. Indeed it seems nothing short of miraculous that the entire series of paintings in St Michael's Chapel in the Convent of the Nuns of the Order of St Clare at Pedralbes (near Barcelona) should have remained so splendidly intact. These paintings, which cover not only the entire wall surface but also the arches and ceiling of a small, irregularly shaped room, are not frescos but murals painted in oils. Ordinarily such painting, when exposed to the air, flakes off or crumbles after a few decades; what is so amazing here is that nothing of this sort has happened, and it would seem that Bassa lit on some process, whose secret is lost, for ensuring the preservation of his colors. Even if we allow for the fortunate circumstance that these paintings were protected for several centuries by tall wooden cupboards (containing the nuns' linen), it is surprising enough that since their discovery nearly fifty years ago the brilliancy of the colors has remained unimpaired. It does not seem that any sort of varnish was employed; more likely some foreign substance was mixed into the oil. In any case they have today a freshness and an almost phosphorescent sheen reminiscent of certain miniatures. Though oil paint seems to have been used from the beginning of the 13th century onwards for decorative ornaments and for embellishing stone figures, and though a contemporary of Giotto, Giorgio d'Aquila, is known to have painted in oils, these murals at Pedralbes are the first examples of wall surfaces thus treated.

In this small chapel (which opens directly on the cloister, with five windows and a door) there is no question of the decoration being adjusted to the structure of the edifice or determined by it; on the contrary, the artist has shown much ingenuity in making the best of the awkwardly arranged and unsymmetrical surfaces at his disposal, and has decorated them in a manner suggesting the altarpiece rather than the mural as we know it. The lay-out, despite these drawbacks, is strikingly successful. On the three main walls the lower row of scenes depicts the Seven Joys of the Virgin: the *Annunciation*, the *Nativity*, the

FERRER BASSA (?-1348). HOLY WOMEN AND ANGEL. DETAIL FROM THE HOLY WOMEN AT THE TOMB (1345-1346).
CONVENT OF PEDRALBES.

(1340). ST FRANCIS OF ASSISI AND ST CLARE (1345-1346). CONVENT OF PEDRALBES.

Adoration of the Magi, Pentecost, the *Ascension*, the *Coronation of the Virgin*, the *Holy Women at the Sepulchre*; to these being added the *Triumph of the Mother of God* (or 'Virgin in Majesty'). The upper tier depicts scenes from the Passion of Christ: the *Garden of Olives*, the *Flagellation*, the *Way to Golgotha*, the *Crucifixion*, the *Descent from the Cross*, the *Pietà*, and the *Entombment*. The scenes follow in chronological order, but the composition is arranged in such a way that, notwithstanding the difference in size between the upper and lower scenes, the center of the panel is filled, above, by the Crucifixion and, below, by the Virgin in Majesty. Though each scene is complete in itself, all are connected in a highly skilful manner; thus to the rocky landscape in the *Adoration of the Magi* corresponds the rock in the *Entombment*. The picture sequence starts on the left, from the central arch, terminating on the right in a corner where four additional rectangular scenes are inserted, the lower ones representing St Francis of Assisi and St Clare—tall, austere figures but strikingly contemporary and 'alive', whereas the other scenes are bathed in the glamour of the legendary past; next come Sts Agnes, Catherine and Eulalia. Above are Sts Michael and John the Baptist, Sts James, Domninus and Honoratus. At the back is an arch painted with decorative motifs and medallions, while on its supports on either side are big figures: Sts Barbara and Isabella, Stephen and Alexis. Above the doorway are two small, particularly graceful figures: St Bonaventura and an angel crowning her with flowers.

In this ensemble, as large and as elaborately constructed as any of the famous Italian frescos, we are struck above all by the artist's descriptive power. The oil technique has the advantage over the fresco that it brings out more clearly the perfect 'finish' of each scene, the exact traits of faces and the emotive quality of the various attitudes. Though obviously

FERRER BASSA (?-1348). ST BONAVENTURA (1345-1346).
CONVENT OF PEDRALBES.

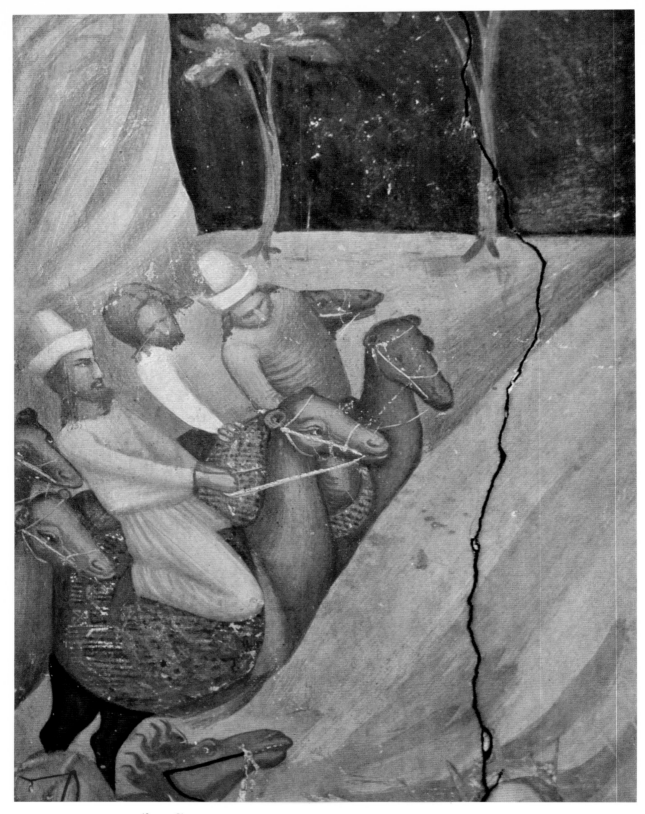

FERRER BASSA (?-1348). THE MAGI. DETAIL FROM THE ADORATION OF THE MAGI (1345-1346). CONVENT OF PEDRALBES.

less refined, the Catalan painter strikes us at once as being much freer and more forthright than his Sienese equivalents. His vision is more spacious and, better than theirs, embraces the composition as a whole. Also he has a gift for choosing between the elements of his narrative and achieving expression by well-placed accents. Thus when we compare, for instance, his picture of St Bonaventura with that (in a similar attitude) of Ambrogio Lorenzetti's St Dorothy, we find that while the Italian excels in his renderings of details, in the delicacy of his drawing and the minute precision of the flowers that figure in the *décor*, the Catalan artist outdoes him in the general movement imparted to the figure, the simplification of forms (for example the garland of roses so clearly indicated with a few deft brushstrokes), the naturalness of attitudes and drapery. Highly effective, too, are the foreshortenings in his renderings of the personages on camels. The posture of the man who is kneeling has been very closely studied, whereas in painting the other two, in the background, the artist has not troubled about perspective and contented himself with painting simple masses of color differing only in the inclination of their planes. The scenes of the Passion have an almost savage intensity and a rugged grandeur very modern in conception. In rendering the same scenes Simone Martini has recourse to complicated gesticulation, charged with emotive overtones. Bassa's composition is much simpler; grief is expressed by the faces of the Virgin, the Holy Women, Nicodemus drawing the nails from the Cross: faces which poignantly reveal an all-consuming inner anguish.

Particularly noteworthy is the expressive value of the hands; we shall see many other examples of this in Spanish art, one of whose most attractive features has always been its exquisite rendering of shapely hands. Primitive as is Ferrer Bassa's art, these details are already given prime importance, though what he aims at is not so much perfection of detail as psychological significance: hands clasped in prayer or wrung in grief, hands tense with strain or contorted in mocking gestures towards the suffering Victim; subtle modulations of the fingers of the angel musicians—in every case we find a different configuration appropriate to its context and in every case the Catalan painter effects an admirable synthesis of the structural pattern and its emotive content.

Even more striking, perhaps, is his draftsmanship and color, and we cannot praise too highly the decorative ability he brings to bear on large surfaces, the materials of garments and drapery being deftly correlated by a host of little touches, while delicately indicated motifs criss-cross upon a shimmering background. He does not merely render details, he bodies forth an *impression*—another proof of Bassa's complete originality. For he leaves far behind that literal precision which often makes primitive art seem stiff and stereotyped. In fact the influences of Giotto, Martini and Lorenzetti are more apparent than real in this extraordinary work. That they should affect the themes and general treatment was only to be expected, considering the prestige of the St Francis legend during this period; yet Ferrer Bassa's genius stands out as unique and non-derivative. Suggestions have been made that he visited Italy; these are unsubstantiated and, anyhow, beside the mark. More plausible is the theory that he had contacts with Avignon, but against this is the fact that Simone Martini went to Avignon only just before Bassa began work at the Convent. There are better grounds for supposing (as suggested by that eminent authority on this painter's work, Father Trens) that Bassa owned or saw some of the miniature reproductions of the works of the Italians which were so popular in Spain during this period (as Byzantine formularies had been two centuries before). This would explain certain procedures, in Bassa's composition especially, which recall those of the Italian masters. But they served the painter as a ground-plan, no more than that. Starting from this, he gave free rein to his native genius and to the coloristic skill he must have developed in those earlier works which have, so regrettably, disappeared. At the dawn of Primitive Catalan art Ferrer Bassa stands out as an inspired precursor, and long years had to pass before any successor worthy of him appeared on the scene.

That the Court of Aragon was already greatly interested in art is evidenced by the extent of Bassa's output and his success. After his death the title of Court Painter went to Ramón Destorrents of Barcelona who, in 1358, painted a retable at Saragossa and to whom two panels of the large retable in the Royal Chapel of Palma (Majorca) have recently been attributed. The work of this painter is being carefully studied and we have now a definite idea of his technique, the result being that several retables hitherto ascribed to the Serras or their studio can safely be given new ascriptions. Much may be hoped of the research work now in progress, for, as things stand, we are regrettably aware of a breach of continuity between the work of Bassa and the Primitive Catalan School whose evolution began with the Serras and culminated with Martorell. There seems every likelihood that the *œuvre* of Destorrents will serve to bridge this gap in our knowledge.

LUIS BORRASSA (?-CA. 1424). ST PETER WALKING ON THE WATER. ALTAR OF ST PETER (1411).
CHURCH OF SANTA MARIA, TARRASA.

CATALAN PAINTING

It seems probable that Italian influence on Spanish art reached its culminating point after Bassa's death, when it made itself so strongly felt at the Court of Avignon, which was in close and frequent contact with Catalonia. The altarpiece of San Vicente (now in the Museum of Barcelona), with its hieratic figure against a gold background and a series of small scenes fitted in around it, is much more reminiscent of the Sienese School than of Bassa's work, lacking as it does the freedom and bold inventiveness of the latter. It may seem strange that the genius of Bassa took so little effect; but the message of a great contemporary work is often misunderstood and sometimes shunned. And, likewise, an art which now strikes us as minor may have seemed more refined during this period, as being more in line with the new Italian fashion then in vogue. In any case Italian influences became predominant during the second half of the 14th century. From now on the achievements of Romanesque, impressive as they were, and even that of Bassa, were deliberately ignored; Catalan painting became a sequence of constantly expanding cycles in which painters, starting off from the legacy of their forerunners, added discoveries of their own and step by step achieved an ever more personal form of art.

In the works of Jaime and Pedro Serra we can see the time approaching when, in the guise of a sort of Mannerism, Italian elegance was to prevail in Catalonia. Though their art is somewhat monotonous, petrified as it were in ceremonious gestures, proffering gifts and so forth, the finesse and sensitiveness of the faces are a redeeming feature. Even in their big altarpieces the Serra brothers have something of the miniature-painter, absorbed in details and anecdotal elements. Their color is bright, illustrative—and commonplace; still, we cannot help being agreeably impressed by their treatment of their models, and the lightness and precision of the brushstrokes delineating features. Despite the exiguity of his means, Pedro Serra sometimes embarked on grandiose themes, as in the large altarpiece at Manresa where the coming of the Holy Spirit is depicted. In isolated figures (e.g. the two saints in the Museum of Vich) his patient heed to detail serves him in good stead. Indeed we often find in Catalonia that the pictures of saints in the predellas have much more life in them than the more elaborate scenes above, which tend to be unduly decorative.

In Lorenzo Zaragoza, a painter famous in his day, we find less of this decorative tendency and a concentration on essentials. No example of his work was known until the ascription to him of the Holy Virgin altarpiece at Jerica. This discovery is important, for here we have a junction-point between the arts of Catalonia, Aragon and the sphere of Valencian influence. Indeed, before coming to Barcelona, Zaragoza spent his youth at Valencia. At Barcelona he joined the Serra brothers' group and made a number of paintings (none of which is extant) in various towns of the Kingdom of Aragon, especially Calatayud and Teruel, before returning to Valencia where he is known to have resided at the close of the 14th century. In the Jerica altarpiece he handles the already hackneyed theme of the Virgin and Child surrounded by angel musicians somewhat more powerfully and majestically than was usual at the time. The large figures of St Martin and St Aguda, however, telling out against the gold background of the side panels, are treated in a manner foreshadowing the supreme achievements of Valencian painting.

This typically Italian suavity is found again in the early work of Luis Borrassá, who inaugurated the second cycle of Catalan painting—a movement of much wider scope than its precursor. In the large retable of Villafranca del Panades (commissioned in 1392), the first work ascribed to him, the pictures illustrating religious subjects are really scenes of the courtly life of the day; in other words, scaled down to the level of the models the painter had before him. An example of this procedure is the 'embroidery lesson,' in which the Wise Virgins grouped round the Virgin have an engaging air of cheerful, almost homely animation. A native of Gerona, Borrassá moved to Barcelona, where his studio seems to have been a hive of activity, and much of the work turned out there has survived.

This enables us to trace the progress of the artist (after a short period under the influence of the Serra brothers) towards a truly personal and original expression of his genius. It is probably in the St Peter altarpiece (in the Church of Santa Maria de Tarrasa), dated 1411, that we see him at his best, in full possession of his powers. In the panel showing *St Peter Walking on the Water*, the perspective of the fishing-boats is handled with consummate ease and the gestures of the fishermen bending over their nets are wonderfully lifelike.

Noteworthy, too, is the composition with its quite unconventional arrangement of the figures, and it is not less successful here, where the artist has aimed at simplicity,

RAMON DE MUR (?-AFTER 1435). THE LAST SUPPER. PANEL OF THE ALTAR OF GUIMERA. MUSEUM OF VICH.

than in the highly elaborate near-by panel, the *Crucifixion of St Peter*. Here we see reappearing, after fifty years' eclipse, some of the distortions found in Bassa's rendering of the Passion: the faces of the brutal characters, the executioners, are enlarged and accentuated so as to convey an impression of savagery, violence or physical effort, and there are expert foreshortenings. In the *Resurrection* (Museum of Barcelona) these characteristics are still more marked. It is of particular interest to discover at this early stage, in Catalonia, what came to be a dominant feature of Spanish art; we shall find it present simultaneously (in a highly developed form) in Valencian art and again, somewhat later, in the work of Gallego, a Castilian, and we might be inclined in these cases to trace the origin of what was actually indigenous to the influence of the German artists then residing in Spain.

The large altarpiece of Santa Clara (1415) and the fragments of the altarpiece of the church at Seva (1418), now in the Museum of Vich, are no less interesting. An intensely dramatic poignancy is imparted to the *Crucifixion*. Other scenes, treated in a more decorative style, are weaker on the whole—they were probably the work of pupils—except for some well-rendered details here and there. Thus in the scene of *St Dominic Rescuing Merchants Shipwrecked in the Rhone*, which depicts, less skilfully than at Tarrasa, a number of men swimming in the river, there is at the top of the composition a beach with a stranded boat and three trees indicated by a few rapid brushstrokes—a whole landscape evoked with admirable terseness.

The last known work by Borrassá, the altarpiece of St Michael at Gerona, contains a scene of high imaginative power. The artist shows us *St Michael Overthrowing the Satanic Host* and in the foreground is a man with bended knees trying to protect his face and almost knocked over by the tempestuous onrush of the fallen angels. Here for the first time a Spanish painter has mastered the rendering of movement, and we realize the ground that has been covered since the placid, static art of Borrassá's early period. No less remarkable is the advance shown in some of the details of the saints and donors; for example in the man writing (in the altarpiece of San Pedro of Tarrasa), a simple form clad in a black mantle, whose whole significance is focussed in the poise of his hand. Sometimes in earlier works a picturesque detail here and there—a pair of exquisitely drawn shoes or an embroidered garment—gave us the feeling of the artist's direct observation of his models, but these details were, so to speak, 'on the side'; we have here an attempt to convey a synthetic statement of a *character*.

A notable achievement of recent research is the identification of Ramón de Mur who long was known as 'The Master of Guimera' (after the name of the village whence came the altarpiece, now in the Museum of Vich, to which he owes his fame), and who took over the lesson of the master—Borrassá—but with an emphasis on style, subordinating effects of modeling and perspective to an almost 'modernistic' juxtaposition of broad planes. Ramón de Mur's stylization is not symbolical or hieratic but dictated solely by the exigencies of the picture *qua* picture. In a panel whose present state is unfortunately too bad for reproduction here, the artist depicts the creation of Eve. (Themes from Genesis, though often used by the Catalan fresco-painters, are extremely rare in the work of the Primitives.) Here the bodies, roughly indicated forms, one issuing from the other, have been reduced to schematic elements of the general structure and, greatly daring, the artist has brought the volumes forward on to the two-dimensional surface. Hardly less striking are the bold simplifications of the landscape, the animals of Paradise, the stretches of water, the pink-and-blue sky fringed with angels.

Bernardo Martorell took over the torch from Borrassá; though lacking his predecessor's driving force, he was a better draftsman and it was he who gave mediaeval Catalan art its most finished form. All his works have a distinctive family likeness and it is odd that their ascription to him was so belated. Indeed it is only quite recently that a study of contemporary records has proved that works hitherto ascribed to an hypothetical 'Master of St George' were really Martorell's. Faces painted by him are easily recognizable, being

BERNARDO MARTORELL (?-1453/55). THE WOMAN OF SAMARIA.
PREDELLA OF THE ALTAR OF THE TRANSFIGURATION (CA. 1447). CATHEDRAL OF BARCELONA.

rounder, very carefully delineated and wearing a pensive expression. The composition is expert, depth is conveyed by tonal modulations, foreshortenings are flawless and every detail is suitably placed and soberly depicted. None the less the general effect is intricate, rich in intimations. True, the meticulous drawing may detract from the liveliness of the figures, but they gain in poetic charm. Thus in the *Martyrdom of St Eulalia* (Museum of Vich) the naked body of the saint has a delicate beauty all its own. In the *Transfiguration* (altarpiece of the Cathedral of Barcelona, ca. 1447), the painter's masterwork, are some

50

BERNARDO MARTORELL (?-1453/55). THE WOMAN OF CANAAN.
PREDELLA OF THE ALTAR OF THE TRANSFIGURATION (CA. 1447). CATHEDRAL OF BARCELONA.

admirable figures in which the poise of the heads and the adroitly arranged folds of the
drapery combine to form an expressive whole, while (in the same altarpiece) certain faces,
those for instance of the bride and bridegroom in the *Marriage at Cana*, have the far-away
look of persons lost in a secret dream, and, incidentally, there are some delightful still lifes.
Everything, down to the least detail, is charged with significance; the woman going her
way, holding her child by the hand, along the road in the background of the *Woman of
Samaria* has the hieratic majesty of a figure by Masolino.

THE CONVERSION OF ST PAUL. PANEL OF THE ALTARPIECE OF BONIFACIO FERRER (CA. 1400).
SAN CARLOS MUSEUM, VALENCIA.

THE SCHOOL OF VALENCIA

The flowering of the School of Barcelona links up with the rise, at the end of the 14th century at Valencia, of a school of painting which was gradually to take the lead in the evolution of Spanish art. After traveling for some time in Aragon and a brief residence in Barcelona which stood him in good stead, Lorenzo Zaragoza returned to his birthplace, Valencia, round about 1376. It is worth while comparing with the work of this original and forceful artist a set of four pictures dealing with the life of St Luke which Saralegui attributes to an old Valencian master, the Master of Villahermosa, and which Gudiol, plausibly enough, ascribes to an uncle of the Serras who is known to have been banished from Barcelona and to have taken refuge at Valencia. Certainly these compositions (which, formal and hieratic as they are, have much grace and tenderness) show some resemblances to Catalan Romanesque and the art of Ferrer Bassa. This Serra, though little older than his nephews, never quite achieved their easy competence and, along with Ramón Destorrents, may be regarded as representative of the transition to a more sophisticated art which took place at the close of the 13th century. Tramoyeres assigned these pictures (which bear inscriptions in the Valencian dialect) to 1350 or thereabouts; probably they should be dated slightly later. Thus it would seem that the origins of Valencian art imply a direct acquaintance with the well-established Catalan traditions, both popular and cultural, in which a feeling for the monumental (characteristic of the Romanesque artists) still persisted. Another direct influence was, doubtless, that of the painters who came to Spain from Italy and Germany.

At the end of the 14th century an eminent Florentine painter, Gherardo Starnina (said to have been the teacher of Fra Angelico), was working at Valencia; he made two stays in Spain and went as far as Toledo. The ascription to him of the famous altarpiece of Bonifacio Ferrer (one of the finest primitive works in the San Carlos Museum at Valencia, and not unworthy of any great Italian of the period) has now been abandoned; its ascription to Lorenzo Zaragoza is equally unfounded. Bonifacio Ferrer, brother of Vincent Ferrer, after losing his wife and after the death, in 1396, of his seven children in an epidemic, entered the Carthusian monastery of Portacoeli. The altarpiece comprises a *Crucifixion* with seven small scenes linked to the wounds of Christ and depicting the *Seven Sacraments*; and two big side panels representing the *Conversion of St Paul* and the *Baptism of Christ* whose daring simplifications strike a contrast with the scenes of the *Crucifixion* and especially with the predella. This depicts the coming of Bonifacio Ferrer, accompanied by his sons, to the monastery, and includes a picture of his wife and daughters praying—a picture of typically Sienese grace and gentleness. Thus it may be that we have here the result of a collaboration between two painters, an Italian and a Spaniard, or the work of a Spaniard who had visited Italy, or an Italian who had become acclimatized in Spain.

At about the same time, between 1394 and 1405, a painter of German extraction, Marsal de Sax, founded a school comprising his son and a great many pupils. He made several large altarpieces, often in collaboration with a great Valencian artist, Pedre Nicoláu. It is hard to distinguish between the respective shares of these two men and though the more extreme distortions may be attributed to the German's hand, it is evident, nevertheless, that he, too, had come under the spell of the languorous, faintly decadent charm of the art then flourishing at Valencia. It is to Marsal de Sax that Post has finally ascribed the *St George* altarpiece now in the Victoria and Albert Museum, London; this vast battle scene (commemorating the victory of Pedro I at Albocacer, near Huesca) shows a gift for composition of a high order, but most impressive are the tall, graceful figures of the celestial apparitions, serene amid the heat and fury of the combatants. Two panels *(Doubting Thomas; St Clement and St Martha)* formerly in the Cathedral of Valencia and now, regrettably, lost, may have been the work of the same painter; they had some of the distinctive features of the 'Expressionism' to which reference has been made. In this case these panels would belong to his last period, the close of his stay in Valencia, and it was about this time that similar tendencies made their appearance in the work of Borrassá at Barcelona.

Tramoyeres and Mayer believe that it was Pedre Nicoláu who painted the altarpiece of the Holy Cross (now in the Museum of Valencia); here, too, each scene has a quite amazing vitality and the surging crowds on every panel vouch for the passionate, high-strung temperament of this brilliant artist. No less in its composition than in its use of color, the School of Valencia manifests a spontaneity, a wealth of imagination and a feeling for movement that sharply differentiate it from the School of Catalonia. Nicoláu was the leading figure of a whole group of painters including such men as Fernando and Antonio Perez and Gerardo Giner who, according to Post, may have been the makers of the panels in Valencia Cathedral.

Little is known about these painters (all the works of Antonio Guerau, though he was so famous in his day and Court Painter to King Alfonso in 1425, have disappeared), and this is all the more regrettable because they undoubtedly pointed the way to two great masterpieces of Valencian art: the *Annunciation* and St Martin's altarpiece, now in the San Carlos Museum. The altarpiece was originally in the Carthusian monastery of Portacoeli, where it stood above an altar presented by Berenguer Marti de Torres in 1443, which may thus be dated a few years earlier. It includes three large panels representing *St Martin on Horseback, St Ursula,* and *St Anthony Abbot.* In all primitive art there are few figures endowed with such grandeur and simplicity, and the composition is a superb example of the art of handling a flat surface as such. For these pictures are strictly two-dimensional and diverse as they are, all the elements are on the same plane: the dappled, delicately shaded gold background, the rich brocades adorned with curious flowers, the dark, loosely fitting tunics falling in broad folds, the soil sprinkled with stylized roses and tiny turkey-cocks. Only the faces stand out: mysterious yet very human faces, wearing a look of pensive meditation touched with melancholy. The sobriety of the triptych of St Martin differentiates it from many other Valencian works of art, whose display of luxury borders on extravagance. Here the only exotic note is struck by the way in which St Martin's hair is treated, with drooping fringes. There is, perhaps, a hint of clumsiness in the hands and the drawing of the horse—a *gaucherie* rarely found in the work of the cultured artists of Valencia. But so exquisite are the colors that this adds a pleasing touch of spontaneity and vigor to the ensemble.

The big *Annunciation* at the San Carlos Museum has much the same characteristics, the same fusion of hieratic feeling and sensibility. But it is obviously the work of a more adroit and sophisticated artist. He imparts a singular expressiveness to the eyes and hands, the latter being of quite exceptional beauty. Saralegui thinks the painter was Fernando or Antonio Perez and entitles him provisionally "The Master of Bonastre"; the Master of Los Marti de Torres, in his opinion, belonged to the same family and was perhaps Gonzalo Perez. However the affinities between the two works are perhaps more superficial than real; the first-named is an organic, well-balanced whole, and the other works attributed to the artist are far from achieving the same superb equilibrium. The second picture, on the other hand, suggests great possibilities of development. This is why Tormo advanced a theory, subsequently endorsed by several other authorities and still championed by Gudiol (taking his stand on similarities of style), that the *Annunciation* was the work of none other than Luis Dalmáu and that he painted it on his return from Flanders. Against this is the fact that we do not find in the *Annunciation* any traces of that direct influence of Van Eyck which is so markedly present in Dalmáu's later work, *The Virgin of the Councillors* painted at Barcelona. The technique of the earlier work, though perfect in its way, is of a less advanced order. The arrangement of these big figures on the gold background has the grandiose simplicity characteristic of the School of Valencia between 1430 and 1440. Thereafter, this kind of composition persisted in the provincial and even the 'folk' art of the region and we also find it, though under a much more elaborate form, in the work of such great artists as Reixach (or Jacomart). There are traces of it even in Bermejo's art.

Two distinct trends, in fact, are perceptible in Valencian painting during the second half of the 15th century. On the one hand, there was a 'learned' form of art incorporating

THE MASTER OF LOS MARTI DE TORRES. ST URSULA, DETAIL. ALTAR OF BERENGUER
MARTI DE TORRES (BEFORE 1443). SAN CARLOS MUSEUM, VALENCIA.

THE MASTER OF LOS MARTI DE TORRES. ST MARTIN, DETAIL. ALTAR OF BERENGUER
MARTI DE TORRES (BEFORE 1443). SAN CARLOS MUSEUM, VALENCIA.

VIRGIN OF THE ANNUNCIATION, DETAIL. DIPTYCH OF THE ANNUNCIATION, RIGHT PANEL.
SAN CARLOS MUSEUM, VALENCIA.

Flemish and Italian technical advances (though it never allowed these completely to predominate); on the other hand, a number of local schools in the outlying districts continued treating sacred themes on more traditional lines, and, while their works show little progress, they have an engaging pungency, a savor of the soil. These schools, our knowledge of which has been much enlarged by Saralegui's researches, stem from the ateliers of Nicoláu and his followers. One of the greatest of these painters was the Master of St Anne, who owes this name to a large altarpiece (which, unhappily, has been destroyed) in the Cathedral of Jativa, in which the modeling of the figures was original and striking. His atelier was the starting-off point of two sharply defined tendencies represented, firstly, by the Master of Jativa, whose figures are more static, and the Master of Los Artes, whose protagonists, gazing heavenwards, seem lost in some rapturous dream. The second of these tendencies is represented by the Master of Perea, whose manner is more hieratic and more rugged. His work must have seemed sadly outmoded in its day (round about 1500); nevertheless it commands our admiration, such is the purity of his line and his complete disdain for foreign influences.

For, during fifty years, a more cosmopolitan art, closely associated with the Court, had been coming into favor; it prepared the way for the Spanish Renaissance, in which Valencia took the lead. This movement was long associated with the name of Jacomart; but though much information regarding his life and output is available and a great number of works have been ascribed to him, none of these ascriptions can be wholly relied on. Jacomart was born in 1410 at Valencia, his family was already in the service of the Crown and when little more than a boy he was employed on confidential missions. On at least two occasions he visited Italy. In 1441 he was at Naples, where he was nominated for the post of Court Painter, and he did not return to Spain until the end of 1445. He visited Italy again in 1446 and was in the neighborhood of Rome when commissioned by the King (July 24, 1447) to paint some banners and a large gonfalon. On his return to Valencia he received orders for various altarpieces and was confirmed in his appointment as Court Painter. He died on July 16, 1461. It is noteworthy, however, that his functions seem to have been chiefly those of, so to speak, an impresario, and that very few works by him are extant. The big Segorbe altarpiece illustrating the life of St Martin, regarded as his major work, was delivered to the church in 1447 and, unless he started it before leaving for Italy, can hardly have been painted by him. It is, perhaps, significant that during this period another painter, Juan Reixach, spent several months at Segorbe, and it is definitely known that the Cati altarpiece, commissioned from Jacomart just before his death, was painted entirely by Reixach.

Thus we may well concur with Saralegui in wondering whether the bulk of the paintings ascribed to Jacomart (or, anyhow, to his influence) should not be referred to Reixach, whose authenticated *œuvre* (unlike Jacomart's) is copious and who would thus become the leading figure of mid-fifteenth century Spanish art. This would explain why, in the work hitherto attributed to Jacomart, Italian influences are far from being as much in evidence as we would have expected, considering the time he spent in Italy. The art of Reixach, with its elaborate *décors*, rich costumes and expressionist figures, is fundamentally Valencian. But here, too, we come against a problem; the name of Reixach crops up at periods and places relatively remote from each other. Thus we are told of a Juan Reixach who had settled at Saragossa in 1431, whereas the collaborator or 'ghost' of Jacomart was working in 1447 at Segorbe, in 1461 at Cati, and in 1468 at Cubells (in Catalonia). Then, again, the same name reappears in 1484. The explanation might be that a father and son are being referred to; still, given the uniformity of the works concerned, there is better reason to suppose that there was only one Juan Reixach, a painter who worked assiduously and conscientiously throughout a very long career. Reixach, in whose works are several pictures of small pieces of sculpture, may have been the son of a Lorenzo Reixach, a sculptor living at Barcelona. He is referred to in 1466 as the King's Painter, he was given many commissions by the Court, the nobility and clergy, and his influence was certainly widespread (Saralegui aptly describes him as "the Master of the little Spanish masters").

LUIS DALMAU (?-CA. 1460). THE COUNCILLORS RAMON VALL AND ANTONIO DE VILATORA.
THE VIRGIN OF THE COUNCILLORS, DETAIL FROM RIGHT PANEL (1445). MUSEUM OF CATALAN ART, BARCELONA.

JAIME HUGUET (?-1492). ST GEORGE AND THE PRINCESS (BEFORE 1448).
MUSEUM OF CATALAN ART, BARCELONA.

HUGUET AND THE LAST PHASE OF THE CATALAN SCHOOL

The first Spanish artist to come directly under Flemish influence and to make known to his fellow-countrymen what he had learnt in the Van Eycks' studio was Luis Dalmáu. Jan van Eyck had been a member of the diplomatic mission sent by Philippe le Bon, Duke of Burgundy, in 1428 to solicit the hand of Isabel of Portugal. The Burgundian visitors made a point of seeing much of the country, took part in a pilgrimage to Compostella and traveled as far south as Valencia and Granada. Engaged in making a portrait of the Princess, Jan van Eyck may not have joined in all these expeditions, but we can be sure he came in contact with many Spanish painters.

In 1431 the King of Aragon sent Luis Dalmáu to study at Bruges. It is highly probable that he was working in the Van Eyck's studio in 1432, at the time when the Saint Bavon altarpiece was being painted, for obvious reminiscences of it can be seen in the altarpiece *The Virgin of the Councillors* (commissioned in 1443, completed in 1446) made by him for the chapel of the municipal council of Barcelona, where on his return to Spain he had settled, after a short stay in Aragon. Both the drawing and composition of this work are thoroughly Flemish. There is a curious ineffectiveness, however, in its color, which led some to question if Dalmáu employed the new procedures invented by the Van Eycks, and to suspect that he merely followed the traditional method of painting in tempera—the method which continued to be followed by the School of Barcelona (and especially by Huguet) for forty years. Recent analyses, however, have shown that this was not the case and that Dalmáu did paint in oils; but the fact remains that, owing perhaps to its lack of brilliancy, this work had little influence on the art of its period (despite the very real beauty it possesses thanks to that traditional Spanish virtue, the exquisiteness of the drawing) and must be regarded as a case apart. The leading figure in Catalan art during the second half of the 15th century was Jaime Huguet, who took up painting exactly where Martorell had left it, almost as if no foreign art had ever intervened in Catalonia.

Huguet's name was rescued from oblivion only in 1880; but since then so much research-work has been done that he now is one of the Spanish artists regarding whom we have the fullest information and whose work can be most positively identified. The process of discovery was none too easy. It has been possible to group a number of lesser works in Catalonia and Aragon around an outstanding one: *St George and the Princess*, in the Museum of Barcelona. Post ascribed this picture and its satellites to a rather mediocre Aragonese painter, Martin de Soria, thus crediting him with a unique, precocious flash of inspiration. On the other hand, it was observed that when Huguet's work made a sudden appearance on the scene in 1448, such was its maturity and craftsmanship that one could hardly assume him to have been a tyro at the time. After this date he settled at Barcelona, commissions flowed in steadily and there are abundant and reliable records of his output during this period. There could thus be no doubt about the authorship of his Barcelona works, and it now was noticed that the pictures hitherto ascribed to Martin de Soria were quite remarkably like them. With the result that in their most recent work (1950) Gudiol and Ainaud, after careful research, have come to the conclusion, backed by solid arguments, that Huguet resided in Aragon from 1440 to 1447 and during this period made all the paintings which had formerly been grouped around the *St George* panel.

Thus the gaps in our knowledge of Huguet's life have been filled up. His birthplace was probably Valls (in Tarragona), and he was a son, or anyhow near relation, of the painter Pedro Huguet who had set up house in Barcelona, near Martorell's studio. It appears that Jaime Huguet studied painting between 1435 and 1440, then moved to Saragossa and worked for various churches in the province. The altarpiece of Cervera de la Ceñada is ascribed to him; also the triptych of Alloza (a hamlet near Teruel), and the altarpiece of St George, whose central panel is in the Museum of Barcelona and the two wings in Berlin Museum. The elongated figures, the faces faintly tinged with sadness, are treated with a notable delicacy of touch; in particular, the Alloza Virgin, wrapped in a huge dark

JAIME HUGUET (?-1492). THE EXECUTIONER'S ASSISTANT. RETABLE OF SARRIA,
ST VINCENT AT THE STAKE, DETAIL. MUSEUM OF CATALAN ART, BARCELONA.

JAIME HUGUET (?-1492). STS ABDON AND SENNEN. RETABLE OF STS ABDON AND SENNEN,
CENTRAL PANEL (1459-1460). CHURCH OF SANTA MARIA, TARRASA.

cloak, recalls, if in a simpler, more 'modern' guise, Borrassá's isolated figures. Huguet brought to perfection the technique of tempera painting as practised by the painters of the frontals and ameliorated by Martorell. The mixing of white into the pigments (of which Huguet used a great variety) renders the colors opaque, the modeling is subtly graduated and the painter has given the eyes of his figures an alertness and vivacity quite exceptional in his day. These works, often on a relatively small scale, show steady progress, and it is natural enough that after a year at Tarragona the painter moved to Barcelona, feeling himself in full possession of his powers and qualified to undertake works on a larger scale. To this transitional period we may doubtless ascribe the small altarpiece of the *Epiphany* which, though unfortunately in very bad condition, is one of the most treasured possessions of the Museum of Vich. It shows the Holy Family surrounded by persons clad in sumptuous garments such as were worn by the nobility; the faces have an unquestionable kinship with those in the early works, in the altarpiece of the *Constable* and the retable of Sts Abdon and Sennen at Tarrasa.

Dalmáu's famous altarpiece of the *Councillors* was finished in 1446. It would seem that no sooner had Huguet returned than Dalmáu launched a campaign against the new procedures imported from abroad, and set himself to prove that by a subtler and more skilful handling of traditional methods he could vie with them. His first Barcelona works —the panel of *St Vincent at the Stake* (retable of Sarria), the large retable of *St Anthony Abbot* (1455-1458) which was burnt with the church of San Antonio in 1909, the *St Michael* altarpiece and the Tarrasa retable (1459-1460)—illustrate the culminating point of his technical development. It must be admitted that, depending wholly on the brilliant crafts-manship of a single artist and somewhat archaic in its form, Dalmáu's 'message' was limited in scope, but these defects, if such they were, are redeemed by its discretion and gentle beauty.

Huguet was involved in the political events of the day and played an important part in them. This was the time of the Catalonian uprising against Juan II of Aragon and his wife Juana Enriquez. The Catalans began by supporting the Crown Prince Carlos de Viana and after his death offered the crown to the King of Castile, and, on his refusal, to Pedro, Constable of Portugal, a descendant of the last Count of Urgel. The Constable landed at Barcelona in 1464, proclaimed himself King of Aragon and, despite the war, inaugurated a brilliant court at Barcelona. Several times elected President of the Confraternity of Painters, Huguet was invited to take part in the decoration of the Royal Palace and given amongst other commissions one for an altarpiece for the Chapel. After the Constable's death in 1466 and that (in 1470) of the new pretender, Juan of Lorraine, who was sponsored by the King of Naples, Catalonia was forced, at the capitulation of Pedralbes, to acquiesce in the return of Juan II. The resulting economic depression was unfavorable to artistic activity. Huguet, however, who had a large staff of apprentices and collaborated with the Vergós family of painters, continued to receive important commissions. He had finished the retable of *St Bernardin and the Guardian Angel* in 1468 and now set to painting that of St Augustine (finished in 1485) of which, however, one panel only, *The Consecration of the Saint*, is by his hand. It seems clear that Huguet died in 1492; he had made his will on February 14 of that year and a document of May 4 speaks of his wife as a widow. In the output of his last period, it is difficult to distinguish Huguet's own work from that of his assistants, and his art is of an 'official' order. The figures are as brilliantly drawn as ever, but the increasingly sumptuous brocades have a cramping effect. Backgrounds are submerged under metal incrustations and carvings and, grandiose as is the structure as a whole, the painted surface is no more than a part of it. This in fact was the end of an art which had been assigning an ever larger place to the labors of the wood-carver, the gilder and other craftsmen, which characterize the Spanish retable in its most gorgeous phase. Moreover by now painting in oils had established itself as the normal technique; its triumph was consecrated in Barcelona, indeed throughout Spain, by the work of a man who carried out what Dalmáu, his forerunner, had merely adumbrated: Bartolomé Bermejo.

JAIME HUGUET (?-1492). ST BERNARDIN PREACHING. RETABLE OF ST BERNARDIN,
DETAIL FROM CENTRAL PANEL (1468). CHAPTERHOUSE OF THE CATHEDRAL, BARCELONA.

THE MASTER OF SOPETRAN. PORTRAIT OF A MENDOZA
(PERHAPS THE MARQUIS OF SANTILLANA OR HIS SON, FIRST DUKE DEL INFANTADO).
PANEL FROM THE RETABLE OF THE HERMITAGE OF SOPETRAN (40½ × 23½"). PRADO, MADRID.

THE ADVENT OF NORTHERN TECHNIQUES

In the 14th century and during the first half of the 15th century Aragon, though politically dominating Valencia and Barcelona, was, from the artistic point of view, merely a meeting-place for the painters of these two great cities which, thanks to their position on the coast, maintained their commercial supremacy. Important commissions usually went to artists hailing from the coastal cities, and these artists found it in their interest to open studios at Saragossa. However there were quite a number of local schools. Though these have been little studied up to now and no front-rank painter has so far been ascribed to them, some works are of undoubted interest: for example, the *Virgin* (1439) in the Lázaro Collection, the work of a follower of Lorenzo Zaragoza, Mosen Sperandeu, and the Arguis altarpiece (ca. 1440) now in the Prado. The drawing in these works is competent, the color vivid; the only notable difference between them and Valencian art being a greater simplicity and, in the last-named work, marked traces of Flemish influence.

It was only to be expected that such influences would make themselves more strongly felt in districts where the local schools had not quite found themselves as yet, and this is even truer of Castile than of Aragon—not to mention Navarre which, governed by half-French princes, was almost a fief of the French crown, besides lying on the route of northern painters making their way to Spain. In any case the range of action of the Catalan and Valencian artists did not extend so far afield, and the taste of the rulers and nobility led them to purchase large numbers of Flemish pictures and to patronize artists coming from abroad or, anyhow, artists who painted in the Flemish manner.

Nevertheless, for the decoration of large religious edifices Italians were still called in. Thus at the end of the 14th century a group of Italians took charge of the decoration of the Cathedral of Toledo, where the frescos in the Chapel of St Blaise, attributed to Gherardo Starnina, came to be regarded as a model of what such work should be. Thus, too, the *Last Judgment*, painted in 1446 by the Florentine Dello di Nicola for the apse of the Old Cathedral of Salamanca, enjoyed vast renown throughout Castile; the Chapter of the Cathedral of Leon ordered, in 1452, a similar decoration and had the painter Nicolás Francés study his model on the spot. These frescos have been destroyed, but a good many altarpieces by this painter have survived, amongst them that of the Cathedral of Leon (1434), whose colors are charmingly delicate and limpid. All the same these huge Italian compositions, with their cosmic pretensions and symbolical nudes, had no permanent effect on Castilian art; they had come too soon and the ground was not sufficiently prepared. Also, no doubt they were fundamentally less to the taste of the inhabitants of this rugged and austere land than was the realistic, descriptive art and forthright piety of the Flemish artists. After Jan van Eyck, one of whose most celebrated works, the *Fountain of Grace*, now in the Prado (unless the picture in the Prado is a copy), was bought by the King of Castile and presented to the Monastery of the Parral, near Segovia, where it was already in 1454, the painters most in favor were Rogier van der Weyden, the Master of Flémalle, Dirck Bouts, Gerard David and Hugo van der Goes. Their works, whether originals or copies, were everywhere to be found in Spain, indeed the Feria of Medina del Campo developed into a sort of Flemish picture-mart.

But it was not in the Spanish temperament to accept seeing the world through foreign eyes. The Flemings were welcomed because they introduced a wealth of technical inventions, but the Castilian painters, after assimilating their procedures, employed them as means for expressing their personal vision. A love of fine craftsmanship is innate in all the painters of the Peninsula and the practitioners of painting in tempera had always excelled in this respect. So much so that before long Spanish artists were being invited to Italy, where they were much admired for their mastery of, and improvements on, the technical discoveries of the Flemish painters.

Jorge Inglés was the first front-rank painter to give a new direction to the procedures of the Flemings and, though his name might suggest that he was of Nordic extraction, he

JORGE INGLÉS. THE MARQUIS OF SANTILLANA.
RETABLE OF THE HOSPITAL OF BUITRAGO (1455). COLLECTION OF THE DUKE DEL INFANTADO, MADRID.

was thoroughly Spanish in his handling of them. It was he who made the retable ordered in 1455 for the Hospital of Buitrago by the Marquis of Santillana, a famous poet and member of the Court of Juan II. This retable is unusual in that the donors, the Marquis and his wife, far from figuring discreetly in the shadow of some sacred personage, occupy the two main panels; they are attended by a page and a maid of honor, and the scene is laid in rooms of their palace, whose furniture and decorations are reproduced in detail. True, the donors are kneeling, but their expression is far from prayerful. The artist shows amazing psychological insight in his rendering of features; the character of that astute, self-willed politician, the Marquis, is brought out by the pinched lips and square, strongly modeled face, while his wife's face is all gentleness, aureoled as it were by the heavy, rounded *coiffure*. One feels that the painter has firmly grasped his subject; the landscapes, glimpsed through two narrow windows, have a strange, timeless limpidity, details are perfectly handled, each assigned its right place, and the same applies to even the most trivial accessories of the costumes, the rich materials, the carpets, the open book and the quaint little dog lying under its mistress's faldstool. No less striking are the four saints on the predella, telling out against a uniform background; though without any attributes to distinguish them, they are thoroughly individualized. Looking at this work we feel that few if any of the world's primitive artists have analysed the psychology of their models so skilfully as Jorge Inglés.

Lafuente Ferrari has detected the influence of Rogier van der Weyden in the copious production of the Master of the Retable of the Benedictine Monastery, Sopetran, in which were included the Scenes from *The Life of the Virgin* now in the Prado. Though the Scenes themselves have little to commend them, the portrait of the donor in one of the panels

is admirably done. This donor is believed to have been a member of the Mendoza family and some have thought to see in him the Marquis of Santillana himself. However, the picture does not seem old enough to justify this view and it is more likely that we have here a portrait of his son, the Duke del Infantado. Here, again, the kneeling figure is wonderfully alive, and equally effective are the lightness of the architecture depicted, the homely simplicity of the members of the household and the loving care with which each detail is treated; for instance, the tiny figures of the retable resting on the altar in the picture. The composition being built up vertically, various distortions and elongations differentiating its style from that of Jorge Inglés have been introduced. Another interesting point is that, as in the Buitrago portraits, the donor is attended (in the middle distance) by another person, possibly a retainer, but much more like a sort of 'double,' so closely (except for looking younger) does he resemble the leading figure. This resemblance is equally pronounced in each of the three works (by two different artists) that we have been considering and the explanation seems to be that in each case the donor wished the portrait to contain more than a likeness of the man he was at the time of its being painted and to place his earlier life, no less than his present life, under divine protection. For, despite their surface realism, we feel that these works are charged throughout with 'hidden meanings' and a spiritual significance.

Very different is the work of the large school that flourished at Avila in the middle of the century and gave vigorous expression to an art racy of the soil. An outstanding work of this school is the triptych of the *Nativity* (1475) in the Lázaro Collection, in which we see an odd combination of the ingenious procedures of Flemish art (e.g. the angels flying above the crib and the tubular folds of the Virgin's mantle) with a rustic inexpertness not

THE MASTER OF AVILA. THE NATIVITY. TRIPTYCH OF THE NATIVITY, CENTRAL PANEL.
LAZARO COLLECTION, MADRID.

devoid of charm. There is tender poetic feeling in the treatment of the Virgin's curls and
a naïve fidelity to life in the forms of St Joseph and the shepherd clad in the coarse
homespun garments of the mountaineers of the Sierra. Other works by this painter (still

FERNANDO GALLEGO (FL. 1466-1507). CALVARY. PANEL FROM AN ALTARPIECE, NOW DISPERSED.
WEIBEL COLLECTION, MADRID.

known as 'The Master of Avila,' though probably to be identified with Garcia del Barco)
can be seen in the churches of Barco and of San Vicente at Avila. To this school probably
belong the best panels of the altarpiece of La Sisla (near Toledo), now in the Prado:

The Circumcision and *The Purification*. Other schools, with the same qualities of youthful vivacity combined with a certain awkwardness, flourished at Valladolid and Palencia.

It was from this favorable soil, so rich in possibilities, that once again there arose a new and vigorous personality, that of Fernando Gallego, who is believed to have been born round about 1440-1445. Outstanding in his large output are the altarpiece of *St Ildefonso* at Zamora Cathedral, made to the order of Cardinal Mella (1467), an altarpiece he completed in 1507 for the Chapel of St Anthony at the New Cathedral of Salamanca, and another, fragments of which are now in the Weibel Collection (Madrid). Gallego worked in many parts of Castile, notably in the environs of Palencia where about 1473 he painted no less than six altarpieces. His influence made itself felt as far afield as Trujillo in Estremadura and on the frontiers of Portugal (in the great altarpiece at Ciudad Rodrigo). His work would give an impression of total realism but for some quite original distortions due to his preoccupation with style. Post associates him with Conrad Witz, but it is probably less a question of influence than a chance resemblance (though Martin Schongauer's prints are known to have had a large market in Spain at this time). Like that of Witz, Gallego's art took form outside the sphere of influence of the Low Countries and in a field little exploited hitherto; hence its freshness and boldness. Much has been said about the distortions Gallego imparts to faces, large bulging eyes and strangely mobile lips, and also his habit of slewing figures round in queer, unlooked-for postures and depicting gestures arrested in mid course. Equally noteworthy is his way of painting garments; under his brush rich brocades lose their stiffness and become lustrous, smoothly flowing elements of the composition. Finally, his renderings of landscape strike us as typically Spanish, inspired it would seem by the great open spaces of the Castilian plateau. In short, Gallego's contribution to Spanish art was salutary and timely, and he had a knack of rejuvenation: taking over the traditional stock-in-trade and stereotyped procedures of his age, he breathed into them new, vibrant life.

A comparison of Gallego's methods of expression with those of his famous contemporary Bermejo is not to the discredit of the former; though he may lack Bermejo's transcendent vision, there is an obvious, indeed remarkable parallelism in the tendencies of both artists towards the exaltation of forms *per se* and their liberation from all conventional significance.

While this Castilian School was developing, Flemish influences percolated to the south and, though with a slight time-lag, came to dominate almost completely a new Andalusian School. These artists profited by the great prosperity of the seaport of Seville following the discovery of America. The rise of this School was rapid; its art was less painstaking and perhaps more superficial than that of Castile, and in it Flemish forms took on a facile charm, an air of sumptuousness. One of its leading figures was Juan Sanchez de Castro, painter of the *Virgin of Grace* and Saints in Seville Cathedral, to whom Post ascribes also the big *St Michael battling with the Devils*, now in the Prado (it was originally in the Hospital of Zafra, a center in close contact with Seville). This is a highly ingenious work, with a dual cycle of celestial and infernal scenes built up round a single commanding figure. The ingenious combinations of animal and human forms in his portrayal of the Satanic host show a remarkable inventiveness on the artist's part.

Another notable Sevillian painter was Juan Nuñez, whose *Dead Christ* with its typically Flemish landscape figures in the Cathedral of Seville. But while the cosmopolitanism of the Seville School was its passport to immediate success, it was also a source of weakness. It was in the old Moorish city of Cordova, less sophisticated and more aloof, and also nearer the East, that the most important Andalusian School arose. Here the procedures already practised by the Catalan and Valencian Schools were studied to good effect, the result being a synthetic art, embodying what was best in both, in conjunction with foreign elements, Italian as well as Flemish. Belonging to this School (which deserves to be better known) were Pedro de Cordoba, Bartolomé Bermejo and, at a slightly later date than theirs, Alejo Fernandez.

BARTOLOMÉ BERMEJO (?-1498). PIETÀ OF CANON LUIS DESPLA (1490).
CATHEDRAL OF BARCELONA.

BERMEJO AND RODRIGO DE OSONA

The most interesting moments in the history of art are those when some great artist, breaking with his forerunners, whether foreigners or compatriots, strikes out for himself. There are, in fact, two sorts of artists: those who fall into line with the past and, if they have strong personalities, continue it to good effect; and, secondly, those who make some drastic change and whose inventions and discoveries are exploited thereafter by their successors. Such was the case of Ferrer Bassa in the early days of Catalan art, and the same was true of Bermejo at the close of the 15th century. A similar claim may be made for Rodrigo de Osona as regards Valencia, though I realize that this claim is made on the strength of one work only that is entirely by his hand—if a large and important one: the *Crucifixion* at the Church of San Nicolás of Valencia—and his share in some other works of outstanding quality in which he was aided by his son.

Greatest of the Spanish Primitives is, unquestionably, Bartolomé Bermejo. His *Pietà* in the Cathedral of Barcelona is signed *Opus Bartholomei Vermeio Cordubensis*, showing that he hailed from Cordova, and it was probably in Andalusia that he acquired his thorough knowledge of Flemish technique. Nothing is known of his life and travels (a signed work by him exists at Acqui in Northern Italy, and some have thought he visited Venetia). He certainly spent some time at Barcelona and in Aragon, and probably at Valencia, and we can picture him as the typical great international artist, unbeholden to any local School. This makes the difference between him and Huguet, whose art is so obviously a summing-up of all Catalan painting.

Bermejo was in Aragon round about 1474, when he was commissioned to paint the retable of Santo Domingo of Daroca, the central panel of which, *St Dominic Enthroned*, is in the Prado. In this work the painter has indulged in all the sumptuous display of the Valencian and Andalusian Schools: gold backgrounds, brocades and sparkling ornaments. He recapitulates almost literally a theme repeatedly employed by Jacomart (or Reixach), but handles it on architectural lines, achieving a strikingly majestic effect. As to the quality of his color, he can vie with that of any Flemish artist, and his technique is certainly superior. The face tells out against a background of white linen and in painting it he displays such power and insight, and handles modeling and chiaroscuro with such skill that a composition which retains the traditional immobility of so much early art suddenly acquires depth and spatial reference. To this period may be assigned the *Santa Engracia* (this Saint was greatly revered in Aragon), now in the Gardner Collection, Boston, and the large *St Michael* in Lady Ludlow's Collection, London, signed *Bartholomeus Rubeus*, i.e. red-haired Bartholomew (*Bermejo* = 'red' in Spanish). Originally in the Church of Tous, a little town in the Valencia region, this work, in view of the disproportion between the saint and the donor, is nearer Primitive art, but the movement imparted to the archangel, the billowing sweep of his cloak, the treatment of the body-armor and materials tell of a great artist already in full possession of his powers. But there is something more: a subtle method of hinting at what lies beyond the picture, which we find in several other works by Bermejo and which constitutes perhaps his greatest claim to fame. Thus on the bulging surface of the saint's cuirass we see a faintly glimmering reflection of distant buildings, a sort of castle or an oriental town with lofty minarets. In other pictures, the *Resurrection* and the *Descent into Hell* (at Barcelona), the figures and the various elements of the landscape are bathed in an indirect light, that of a setting sun outside the margin of the picture.

Bermejo's masterwork, the *Pietà*, commissioned by Canon Despla and completed on April 23, 1490, is in the Cathedral of Barcelona. It is remarkable not only for the effectiveness with which the leading theme is handled, but also for the suggestive value given to its whole setting: to the landscape, architectural features, incidental figures, indeed to the smallest details of the composition. Thus the donor's face, telling of a touchingly sincere and humble piety, with its unkempt, half-grown beard (in striking contrast with the rosy smoothness of the clean-shaven face in the *St Dominic*), stands out against a background of dark rocks and curious vegetation round which butterflies are fluttering. The anguished face of the Virgin has a simple, very human pathos; that of the dead Christ a realism that almost takes our breath away. Above it is a strange crown wrought in gold almost identical with the crown Christ wears in the *Ecce Homo* at the Museum of Vich. Compelling as are these sacred presences, our gaze is drawn away towards a twofold landscape; on one side, perched on a jutting crag, is a windmill delineated with loving care, and on the other a large town, bathed in a reddish glow. On the left, at the foot of the grotto of the sepulchre a soldier is asleep; on the extreme right, on a hilltop, a woman is seated in front of her house in an attitude of sadness. Even Mantegna never rendered architecture more impressively; even Giorgione's details are not more delightful, more mystery-laden; even Patinir's landscapes not more fully realized—the many-sided perfection of this work is all Bermejo's.

Indeed a comparison with Giorgione inevitably suggests itself; if we ignore the holy figures in the foreground (not that we question in any way their importance), we find that

BARTOLOMÉ BERMEJO (?-1498). PORTRAIT OF CANON DESPLA. DETAIL FROM THE PIETÀ (1490).
CATHEDRAL OF BARCELONA.

BARTOLOMÉ BERMEJO (?-1498). LANDSCAPE, DETAIL FROM THE PIETÀ (LEFT SIDE).
CATHEDRAL OF BARCELONA.

the second scene is a quite amazing anticipation—by several decades—of that famous *Tempest* in the Academy of Venice. Here, too, on the left, we have a soldier armed, like Giorgione's, with a long pike. On the right we have not that inexplicable woman suckling a child, but a figure which we may be sure is no less symbolic, a sort of effigy of Wisdom placed in front of the town at a little distance from it. The leading theme is the storm, but divided here into two parts, owing both to the greater expanse of the scene and to a duplication of the thematic structure, a device peculiar to Bermejo and often used by him. The storm is breaking on the left in a welter of greenish clouds, while the gleam of the lightning-flash, or the glow of a fire that it has kindled, lights up the right-hand section of the landscape, the town. Few pictures have given rise to so much speculation as Giorgione's, and Eugenio d'Ors offered a brilliant and colorful interpretation of it shortly before the recent war. However, interesting as are the speculations to which such 'problem pictures' as Giorgione's and Bermejo's may give rise, we will confine ourselves to pointing out that, for many leading painters of the period, the ostensible subject was often merely a pretext for illustrating some other more vital theme whose symbols, known at the time to a small group of initiates, remain a mystery to us; and that Bermejo's art, like Giorgione's, often functions on another than the obvious plane.

In Rodrigo de Osona's *Crucifixion* at the Church of San Nicolás of Valencia, commissioned by Juan de Albarraci in 1476, we have another work in which the creative genius of its maker reveals itself under a great variety of aspects. There is no denying Osona's debt to Italy, where already the technical discoveries of the Flemings had been assimilated. Here the painter has inset in the predella small subjects inspired by antique art, treated in monochrome and giving the illusion of relief, after the fashion of the School of Padua; whereas his scenes of lofty buildings and seascapes with tall ships seem more reminiscent of the art

BARTOLOMÉ BERMEJO (?-1498). LANDSCAPE, DETAIL FROM THE PIETÀ (RIGHT SIDE).
CATHEDRAL OF BARCELONA.

of Flanders. Yet may not he equally well be recalling here the Valencian scene, with its slender, graceful houses, its lush vegetation and its vistas on the sea? In a very striking work by Rodrigo de Osona *fils* (it is known that father and son collaborated over a long period), we find what are undoubtedly features of the landscape of La Huerta near Valencia: peasants' cottages *(barracas)* with the same curved, thatched roofs that can still be seen in Spain today.

Indeed Rodrigo de Osona, too, discovered for himself a style enabling him to excel the works of his predecessors, estimable though these were, and he did this by making a sort of synthesis of their most valuable discoveries. The *Crucifixion* at the Church of San Nicolás belongs to that category of pictures in which an incident familiar to religious art is depicted not only at its climax but in its successive phases, presented simultaneously. Though the persons in the middle distance are carrying the conventional attributes—the executioner's assistants, ladders; Veronica, the veil—and are thus easily recognizable, the composition as a whole is subtly charged with overtones; thus the rising road symbolizes the upward path to be climbed by the aspiring soul and the ship suggests voyages of discovery. Some of the warriors in the middle distance, despite their armor, have reminiscences, unusual at this date, of classical antiquity. Many elements of this work reflect the general conceptions of Valencian art; the extreme slenderness of the Divine Victim, the way faces and hands are 'caught' in the moment of maximum expressiveness, the elegant postures and the delicate renderings of features are typical. Nevertheless, the work as a whole shows the impact of new conceptions and follows a predetermined compositional scheme. Details are merged into the pictorial architecture and the faces of the old men at the foot of the Cross remind us of those "compact human blocks" of which Focillon speaks, with reference to Piero della Francesca.

Lastly, *The Crucifixion* serves as a key-work, comprising as it does a great variety of details and characteristic elements which enable us to link up many outstanding works with the school of this great artist. Thus the three panels in the Johnson Collection, Philadelphia: *The Mourning over the Death of Christ, The Resurrection* and *The Agony in the Garden*, to which Post has devoted much study, have such obvious similarities with the Valencia picture that we can hardly fail to see in them the hand of the elder Osona; illustrations of these similarities are the path leading down to the Tomb, the figure of St Peter in the Garden of Olives (so much like the St Peter of the Valencia predella), the characteristically fan-shaped trees, the seascapes and ships in the background. Rodrigo de Osona, the son, a good many of whose works have been identified, does not quite achieve that inspired detachment which leads an artist's creations to acquire a life of their own, independent both of the artist and their models, and to body forth the loftiest emotions. In the younger Osona's work, though the expressions of the faces have a direct, simple and sometimes poignant appeal, the feelings behind them are of a lower order, earthbound. Despite some superficial resemblances, *The Virgin of the Caballero de Montesa* (Prado) seems to me in a different vein and I question if it should be ascribed to either of the Osonas, the father or even the son. The delicacy and poetic feeling imparted to the figures have led to a certain attenuation of the general effect, while the attitudes, with all their grace, carry a suggestion of the anecdotal. The theory, based on its affinities with a signed picture in the National Gallery, London, that this may well be a work by a member of the group centering on Paolo di San Leocadia (an excellent Italian artist who settled at Valencia and had many disciples) seems more plausible.

We owe it to the diligent researches of Madurell, Ainaud and Verrié that one of the most baffling problems in the history of Spanish painting has now been solved: that of the authorship and date of the famous *Martyrdom of St Cucufas*, originally in the Monastery of San Cugat, and now in the Museum of Barcelona. No less interesting than the main subject of this picture, which represents the beheading of the saint with gruesome realism, are the portraits of the three distinguished persons on the right and the landscape faithfully depicting the Monastery of Cugat as it then was (and still is), instead of some mythical mediaeval town, as was the usual practice in such compositions. For a long while this picture was ascribed to a so-called ' Master Alfonso ' assumed to have been the artist Alfonso de Cordoba who was employed on work at the Royal Palace of Barcelona and commissioned in 1473 to make a retable for the Monastery of Cugat. Were this date correct we should be compelled to see in the *Martyrdom* an entirely new departure, far ahead of its times; such are the gifts of realistic observation and psychological insight it evinces. But documents now have come to light which prove that the San Cugat retable, of which this panel was a part, was painted between 1502 and 1506 by a painter of German extraction whose name (Hans or Heinrich Brün or Brun) was transformed by the Catalans into 'Anye Bru.' Obviously the freedom of treatment we see in this work would be amazing were it contemporary with the tall, stiff figures clad in sumptuous robes and the aureoles in high relief which characterize Huguet's last period and the output of the school of the Vergós. As it is, we must regard this work as a normal manifestation of the international style which came in with the rising tide of the Renaissance at the turn of the century. Not that this detracts at all from the intrinsic value of the picture, which remains a striking testimony to the rapid progress of the new ideas in Spain and the disappearance (speedier at Barcelona than at Valencia) of local particularities.

Thus the art centers of the various Spanish provinces—Catalonia, Valencia, Aragon, and also Castile and Andalusia—lacked neither a diversity of talent nor artistic personalities of striking originality. Moreover, as we have seen, while sometimes affected by foreign influences, the various Spanish schools presented certain dominant characteristics even at this early date which justify us in speaking of a distinctive, homogeneous Spanish art, based on a constant quest of reality and its no less constant sublimation on to the spiritual plane.

ANYE BRU. MARTYRDOM OF ST CUCUFAS, DETAIL.
HIGH ALTAR OF SAN CUGAT (1502-1506). MUSEUM OF CATALAN ART, BARCELONA.

THE RENAISSANCE

★

PEDRO BERRUGUETE AND THE DAWN OF THE RENAISSANCE

ALEJO FERNANDEZ

ROMAN AND LEONARDESQUE INFLUENCES AT VALENCIA AND SEVILLE

MORALES AND MANNERISM

THE COURT PAINTERS OF KING PHILIP II

RIBALTA

YAÑEZ DE LA ALMEDINA (FL. 1506-1536). ST CATHERINE. (83½×44″)
PRADO, MADRID.

THE RENAISSANCE

EVEN in works imbued with the sincerest religious emotion the Primitive Italian artists always manifested in their backgrounds, by way of reminiscences of Greek or Roman architecture, their yearnings for the classical beauty that had left the world. But soon the teachings of St Francis, destined to have so marked an influence on the evolution of art, led to a change of heart throughout the West, and the first and simplest of the lessons inculcated by the Saint was a love for nature and for all God's creatures. Later, in the mid-15th century, Italian painting came to be dominated by the new conceptions of light and perspective. At the same time the beauty of nude bodies was rediscovered and we witness a steadily increasing incursion of 'pagan' elements into even the most sacred themes—its most striking illustration being Michelangelo's *Last Judgment* in the Sistine Chapel. Raphael and his Roman disciples, alongside Leonardo and his Lombard School, helped in promoting a new type of classical ideal which soon won general acceptance throughout Europe.

After assimilating the message of the Flemish painters, Italian art continued this unifying movement, which also (it must be admitted) entailed a loss of spiritual values, a general leveling-down, and the consequences were not always happy, however congenial to the artists were the means of expression this new language put at their disposal. While there is no question that the Italian Renaissance brought a new beauty into the world, along with a host of discoveries as precious as they were unprecedented, we are bound to recognize that it was not always the artists we most admire today who exerted the most influence, nor the worthiest part of their message which took effect. What the artists of the High Renaissance thought to learn from Michelangelo, Leonardo and, above all, Raphael—as interpreted by his Roman disciples—was not necessarily the best in them; in fact, dazzled by the compelling genius of these great men, their contemporaries never really understood them. When we consider the ineffectiveness and servility of the imitations of their works, we realize how salutary was the Venetian reaction against them, and can understand why El Greco railed so fiercely against Michelangelo.

The dawn of the Spanish Renaissance ushered in a great artist who assimilated the Italian message when it had hardly taken form, and, striking out on lines of his own, sacrificed none of the national characteristics. This great artist was—Berruguete. Next, at Valencia, a soil long permeated with Italianism, there arose a group of painters who began by yielding wholly to the influences of Raphael and Leonardo, while in Andalusia and Estremadura, extremist and mannerist influences made themselves strongly felt.

Yet great as always was the prestige in Spain of the Italian artists, it is clear that the new spirit in Italian art evoked no deep response in the Peninsula. On the contrary we find that the profound religious sentiment of Spain, far from succumbing to the lures of pagan forms or affecting a learned humanism, gained strength throughout this period. True, the Spanish artist felt called on to abandon the naïve, anecdotal and descriptive features of religious art which had been in favor during the Middle Ages, but this was not because they struck him as being childish or outmoded, but because they now proved inadequate to meet the demands of a religion ever more intensely felt and tending more and more to a mystical renunciation of all non-essentials and a more spiritualized concept of Catholicism.

This, too, is why, after having seemed to assimilate during the period preceding the Renaissance the elements of a vast, cosmic conception of art's function, and though some powerful and highly original Spanish artists flourished at the close of the 15th century, Spanish art abruptly narrowed its scope. After Bermejo, Osona and Berruguete, who rank amongst the world's greatest painters and whose work seemed so rich in promise for the future, there came a break of continuity, while the artists cast about for ways and means of bodying forth their mystical vision of man and the universe. The 16th century is studded with unavailing attempts in this direction; until at last the problem was solved, if on greatly differing lines, by those three great painters: El Greco, Velazquez and Zurbaran.

BERRUGUETE AND THE DAWN OF THE RENAISSANCE

The personality and works of Pedro Berruguete are coming to take an ever larger place in art history—which is as it should be. He was essentially a man of the 15th century, his life was short and—apart from early works carried out under special conditions, in collaboration with foreign artists—what has come down to us of his output falls within a very short period, from 1495 to 1504. Fortunately his *œuvre*, as enriched by recent discoveries, is copious, and it evidences both a remarkable homogeneity and a complete mastery of his powers. The period of its flowering was a crucial one in Spanish history. The reign of Ferdinand and Isabella, which had brought about the unification of Spain, was drawing to an end. With the marriage of Philip of Austria and Joanna the Mad began that phase of high adventure which was to carry the arms of Spain throughout Europe—for her greater glory and, perhaps, her ultimate ruin—and to prepare the way for the Empire of Charles V. It was now that the institutions of imperial Spain took their final form. The recently established Inquisition had its first great inquisitor-general in Tomás Torquemada, who, it seems, was the moving spirit of the vast decorative program at the Church of Santo Tomás of Avila, chief scene of Berruguete's activities. That great cardinal and adroit statesman, Francisco Ximenes de Cisneros, Primate of Spain from 1496 to 1517, restored the Cathedral of Toledo, where Berruguete did much decorative work (most of which is lost).

No less important events were taking place in the world of art than in that of politics and here, too, Berruguete was in the thick of them. For, being in Italy at this time, he became acquainted with the work of the greatest contemporary inventor of new forms, Piero della Francesca, and quite possibly with the artist himself, with whom he may have worked. In any case he collaborated with Melozzo da Forli and Signorelli, Piero's immediate successors, during that early period of the Renaissance which was perhaps more significant, richer in brilliant promise than even the High Renaissance.

From documents collated by one of his descendants (for a law-suit) we learn much about Pedro Berruguete. He came of a Biscayan family. His grandfather settled at Paredes de Nava, north of Palencia, where Pedro was born in or about 1450. Gallego was working in this part of Spain during the formative years of the young painter, who was thus enabled to see for himself how Flemish techniques could be put to the service of Spanish art. Indeed it would seem that Berruguete as a quite young man had thoroughly mastered all the new procedures. It was on the strength of this accomplishment that he was invited to Italy and commissioned to paint the hands of the Duke of Montefeltro in the famous Brera altar picture of Piero della Francesca, in which the Duke is shown praying to the Madonna. And when he collaborated with Justus of Ghent, at Urbino, he was regarded, Spaniard though he was, as the expert *par excellence* in the techniques of the North. One of Pedro's uncles was a Dominican monk who had associated with dignitaries of the Church in Italy and Spain, and this may partly explain why Pedro stood in such high favor with that powerful religious Order.

He made a fairly long stay in Italy, most of it at Urbino in the service of Duke Federigo, fervent art-lover and patron of Piero della Francesca. But, judging by certain characteristics of his subsequent work, he must also have visited Venice, Rome and perhaps Ferrara, where Cosimo Tura was working. Mention is made in the archives of Urbino of the presence of one "Pietro Spagnolo" on April 14, 1477; almost certainly this refers to Berruguete. But the most important token of his presence there consists in the many paintings he made in the Duke's study at the Palace of Urbino. The Duke had decided to employ the best oil painters of the day for adorning this room with pictures of the most eminent philosophers, judges and doctors of Greece and Rome, and the Old and New Dispensations; and his choice fell on Justus of Ghent and Berruguete. The learned Belgian Hulin de Loo wrote a study of this joint enterprise and Post, after a careful and thorough comparison of these figures with Berruguete's work in Spain, has succeeded in determining which of the Urbino pictures are by his hand. There are a great many of these, amongst them being the famous portrait of the Duke with his son Guidobaldo. Such of the panels as are still in Italy have been installed in

PEDRO BERRUGUETE (CA. 1450-1504). ST DOMINIC AND THE ALBIGENSES.
FROM AN ALTARPIECE IN THE CLOISTER OF SANTO TOMAS, AVILA. (66½×30¾″) PRADO, MADRID.

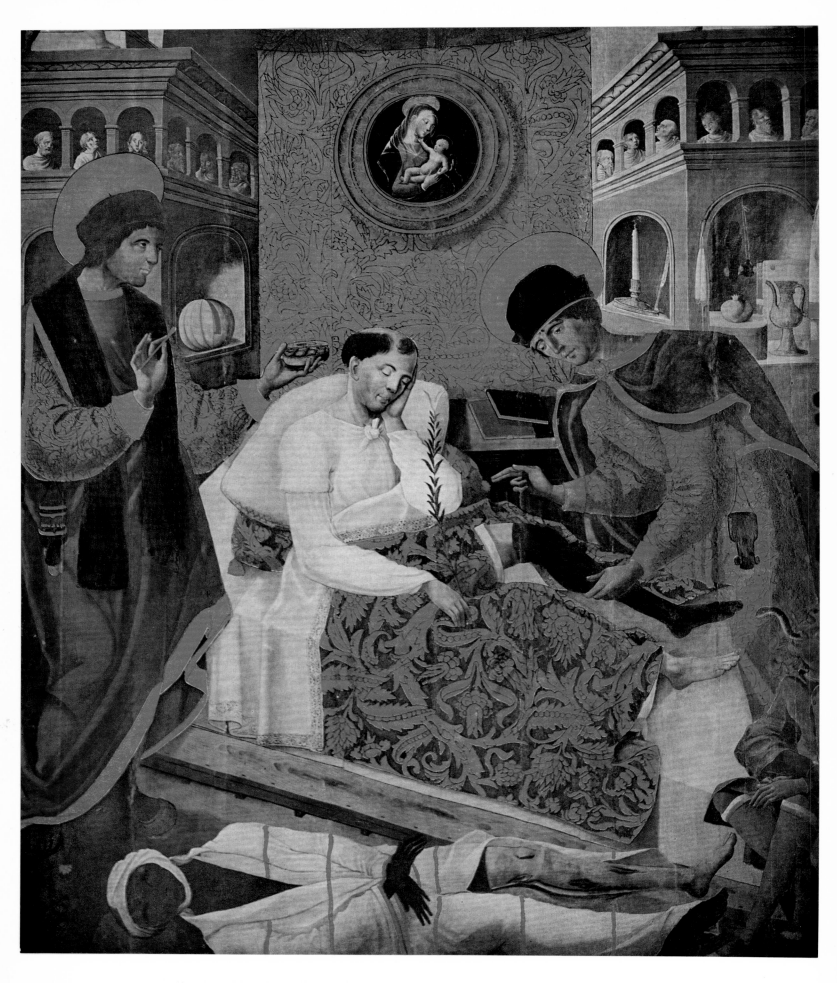

(?) FERNANDO DEL RINCON (?-1518). THE MIRACLE OF SAINTS COSMAS AND DAMIAN.
FROM SAN FRANCISCO DE GUADALAJARA. (74½×41″)
PRADO, MADRID.

the Gallery of the Urbino Palace. Others are at the Louvre. Likewise, four of the seven figures illustrating the 'Liberal Arts' (made for the Duke's library) are now ascribed to Berruguete, and the view that Melozzo da Forli did the sketches for them has been abandoned.

The Duke died in 1482, and his death probably led to the dispersal of his artists. Thus Berruguete is known to have been back in Spain in 1483, the year when Raphael was born; in Urbino, as it so happened. Soon after his return Berruguete married Elvira Gonzales, by whom he had six children, one of them, Alonso, destined to become a famous sculptor.

From now on the painter was employed on work at the Cathedral of Toledo. Though none of the frescos he made there from 1483 on for the Chapel of the Sagrario and in 1495 for the cloister remains, a fresco of the latter date in the entrance of the Chapel of St Peter has survived. His work at Avila, however, has fared better, and constitutes a truly impressive *ensemble*. First we have the retable of the High Altar at the Church of Santo Tomás, with scenes from the life of St Thomas; the bold precision of its drawing and its expert chiaroscuro were something completely new in Spain. However, unlike the Flemings, Berruguete did not eschew the traditional procedures of the Spanish artists, which they had brought to an almost unbelievable perfection as regards the use of gold and silver for ornaments and backgrounds. This is why, at first sight, these pictures seem somewhat akin to those of the Primitives. But on closer inspection, especially of those great isolated figures, prophets and saints, which give the predella of the altarpiece its exceptional interest, we find that here is nothing short of a new conception of the human personality. Berruguete also made two large altarpieces for the Dominican Convent of Avila, dedicated to St Thomas and St Peter Martyr. These panels, now at the Prado, though somewhat uneven in quality (owing probably to the fact that pupils took part in painting some of them), contain some vividly realistic scenes such as the *auto-da-fé* or bonfire of heretical books, ostensibly in the period of the struggle with the Albigenses (in the 13th century), but probably very much like the *auto-da-fés* decreed by the Inquisition in Berruguete's time. In these scenes the composition is remarkable for the skilful handling of perspective, accuracy of proportions, and use of striking light effects, such as a sunbeam falling aslant across the picture to light up St Peter's tomb. In the crowd scenes, the diversity of the types of persons and the way in which their attitudes are arranged suggest that almost mathematical schematization of which Piero della Francesca had given an example. In this connection we may recall those purposive distortions by which some very early Spanish masters sought to enhance the expressive quality of their work. But what in their case was incidental and empirical has become systematized in Berruguete's art, though he abandons these methods when he turns to depicting highly animated scenes. Elsewhere, however, he shows a marvellous ability for locating in space, within long, well-balanced architectural recessions, figures of a massive, monumental quality, static and statuesque. Indeed no Spanish painter before him had so exact a sense of volumes—and none was worthier to beget the most illustrious of Spanish sculptors.

Many works now identified as Berruguete's have been discovered at or near his birth-place. At Paredes de Nava itself, besides the altarpiece of St Eulalia whose predella includes big figures of the Kings of Israel resembling those of the Judges at Urbino, and scenes in which women are depicted with quite Italian grace, there are the remains of another altarpiece dedicated to St Helena, and a large panel of *St Peter Martyr*. The Bishop's Palace at Palencia contains the panels of an altarpiece, originally at Becerril de Campos, illustrating the life of the Virgin—a masterpiece of realism combined with architecturally ordered composition —and four scenes (from the Church of Santa Maria de Flechilla) whose inspiration, on the contrary, is typically Flemish. There are other works by Berruguete in the provinces of Burgos and Segovia; amongst them being a *Decollation of the Baptist*, originally in Santa Maria del Campo, on which the painter has inscribed the monogram of the Duke of Urbino, and a *Salvator Mundi* (Parish Church, Guaza de Campos) dated 1501. Finally, the Lázaro Collection at Madrid owns a portrait of a young man which, though it may not be as once was thought a self-portrait, reveals an interesting attempt to bring out with total sincerity the psychological make-up of the model.

Echoes of Italian art are often to be found in these works; while carefully recorded, the drawing of the faces tends to fall in line with the classical lay-out practised, for example, by Carpaccio. We find them also in the settings, where the artist renders architectural elements in a hueless *grisaille* which not only shows his clean-cut drawing to advantage but also forms an admirable framework for the decorative elements: curtains and garments in bold colors inlaid with gold and spangled with glints of bronze or silver in the traditional manner of Spanish painting. Thus, disciplined as Berruguete's art may be, it never lapses into aridity.

When he died, on January 5, 1504, he had begun work on a retable for the High Altar of the Cathedral of Avila; it was completed by his usual collaborators: to begin with, Santa Cruz (an intriguing name, perhaps the Spanish sobriquet of some Italian artist), then Juan de Borgoña, a painter who had worked at Florence, perhaps in Ghirlandaio's *bottega*, and was employed on the decoration of the Cathedral of Toledo, where some large, rather conventional frescos and a *Last Judgment* in the Sala Capitular of the Cathedral are by his hand. For nearly fifty years the School of Juan de Borgoña flourished in Toledo (where Pedro Machuca, a painter in the Roman manner, was also working) and it ensured the triumph of the Italian style of painting. Prominent members of this group were Francisco and Antonio de Comontes, Pedro de Cisneros and Juan Correa de Vivar whose style closely resembles that of Juan de Juanes but whose color has the coldness favored by Morales.

One artist, however, calls for special mention: Fernando del Rincón, whose achievement, though less impressive than Berruguete's, ran parallel with his. He hailed from Guadalajara and oddly enough his career gave rise to the legend of a great painter of the Catholic Kings, Antonio del Rincón, a purely mythical figure. Now that the mystery has been cleared up, Fernando del Rincón is given an interesting, if more modest, place in Spanish art. Though for some time he held the post of 'Superintendent of Paintings' in Castile, he chiefly worked in his hometown and at near-by Alcala de Henares, birthplace of the great Cardinal Cisneros. Two large portraits by him are extant: of Francisco Fernandez de Cordoba (Governor of Toledo in 1519) and Fray Francisco Ruiz, a friend of Cisneros, appointed Bishop of Avila in 1514. These portraits were something new in Spanish art: the painter treats the faces in large masses, effecting at once a telling simplification and a synthesis, and stressing character-revealing traits.

Agreeing with Tormo, Sánchez Cantón also ascribes to this painter the big panel representing the *Miracle of Saints Cosmas and Damian*, now in the Prado, on the strength of its having been in the Franciscan Monastery at Guadalajara. Post feels less sure about this ascription, though recognizing that the way the saints' faces stand out from the composition tells in its favor. In this picture there is a curious blending of elements of Renaissance architecture with the lavish use of gold practised by Berruguete. Under arcades in the upper part of the composition are small busts in the 'antique manner' (probably representing famous physicians), while below are various objects of common use, treated as still lifes. Thus realistic elements are set off against the symbolical *motifs*.

ALEJO FERNANDEZ

We are better justified in regarding the most notable of the Andalusian masters, Alejo Fernandez, not as a belated Primitive, but as a pioneer of the Renaissance movement, and the awkwardness and unsureness of his style as due to his working at a relatively great distance from the chief centers of Italian humanism. This painter, too, may possibly have been of German extraction, for there is mention in the ledgers of the Cathedral of Seville of Alejo Fernandez under the style of '*Maestro Alexos, Pinctor Aleman*'. Against this is the fact that the names of his parents, Leonisio and Juana Garrido, are thoroughly Spanish, and there are no other indications that he had foreign blood in his veins.

Alejo Fernandez makes his appearance in the last years of the 15th century, at Cordova, where he married the daughter of one of the city's leading painters. We have already mentioned the part played by Cordova as a training-ground for artists, and in the acclimatization in Spain of foreign painters. Bermejo hailed from this city and it was the home for a time of the Flemish artist Pedro de Campaña and of Valdes Leal. Thus the artistic climate of Cordova did much to crystallize the temperaments of artists who had not yet quite 'found themselves,' while Seville, then enjoying a period of great prosperity thanks to her busy commerce with the New World, was a place where artists could count on a ready market for their works and the local studios multiplied and prospered accordingly.

In 1508 Alejo Fernandez was called upon by the Chapter of the Cathedral to carry out some important work, including the decoration of the High Altar, and now began the painter's rise to fame and wealth. The contracts that came to him in a steady flow and other records of his activities enable us to trace his career with some completeness. However, we need not linger over the incidents of his private life, his marriages, the births and deaths of his children and so forth; of greater interest is the picture the records give us of the life of a successful painter in a rich commercial city of the period, where, in the absence of a royal court, a well-to-do middle class ensured the prosperity of the artists. We learn that Fernandez, besides having a very large, well-appointed studio, possessed a big private residence and a number of Indian and Negro slaves whom he treated with the utmost kindness. An affable, cultured, and religious-minded man, he was liked and trusted by the learned prelates attached to the Cathedral and by the directors of the great institutions which were now being founded in Seville; by Maese Rodrigo Fernandez de Santaella, founder of the College of Santa Maria de Jesus (precursor of the famous University of Seville) and Don Sancho de Matienzo, head of the organization appointed to supervise the exploration and exploitation of the New World.

All the most important works by Alejo Fernandez belong to the first third of the 16th century, though the painter's death did not take place until 1543. His fame, which extended not only to northern and eastern Spain but as far as Portugal, was based in particular on his decoration of the Franciscan Chapel erected by Sancho de Matienzo at his birthplace, the village of Villasana de Mena (Province of Burgos): a decoration intended to conjure up the smiling grace of Andalusia in the rugged uplands of the North.

It is in the work of his first period, at Cordova—corresponding roughly to the period when Berruguete was working at Avila—that we find most striking indications of the influence of the new trends in art. True, the figures are placed in huge architectural settings in the 'antique' style, with long recessions whose perspective is rendered with extreme accuracy. But the delicacy of the brushstrokes lends a touch of poetry to even the most mathematically worked-out passages, and, by the same token, gives the slender figures a wholly Umbrian grace. Noteworthy in the *Christ at the Pillar* (Museum of Cordova), a typical work of this artist, is the difference of scale between the figures, a disproportion which cannot be due to inexpertness, considering the correct handling of perspective in the work as a whole. It was in fact a habit of this painter to exalt the central figure—Christ or Virgin—in this manner, and thus to stress its poetic or transcendental significance and its pre-eminence over the human elements: donors, saints or worshippers. We find the same procedure in the beautiful retable of Maese Rodrigo (in a small chapel near Seville Cathedral), dedicated to the Virgin under the aspect in which she is worshipped in this city—as she appeared to Fernando the Catholic during the siege and reconquest—and in which she figured on the 'mascot' of the Conquistadors. Another instance of this procedure is the famous *Virgin of the Navigators*, in which the Virgin is spreading her cloak over a fleet of caravels and a group of kneeling figures, one of whom, the man seen side-face on the left, may possibly be Christopher Columbus. Towards the close of his career (when his work became all but indistinguishable from that of his disciples) Alejo lapsed into a Mannerism in which, despite recourse to systematic distortion and bold stylistic innovations, his creative power frittered itself away.

ROMAN AND LEONARDESQUE INFLUENCES AT VALENCIA

Nevertheless it was from Italy that the material for building up the new art forms was taken over. Two painters, both natives of La Mancha, Hernando Yañez de la Almedina and Hernando Llanos returned in 1506 to Spain after a long stay in Italy. The collation of two documents has established the fact that one of them was working with Leonardo when he was making *The Battle of Anghiari* for the Signoria of Florence. In 1506 these two painters, who at this time usually worked together, collaborated in making an altarpiece for one of the altars at the Cathedral of Valencia, and next year they contracted to make the doors for the High Altar, which had been destroyed in a fire. Both the dimensions and the quality of this work, which was completed in 1509, are quite exceptional. It consists of two gigantic doors which can be opened and closed only with the help of two long poles, spanning as they do the full height of the altar. There are twelve scenes with life-size figures, arranged in three tiers, representing the Joys of the Virgin and the six outstanding events of her life. The settings are peaceful landscapes in which some features of the Valencian countryside are recognizable: for instance, the unusual-looking tower topped with a campanile belonging to the Cathedral of Valencia. Much architecture figures in these scenes, including monuments of classical antiquity and even ruins, while in other panels we see contemporary Spanish houses. The leading figures are clad in plain tunics falling in broad folds, indicating the artist's desire to strike an 'antique' note; shepherds and peasants, however, are treated more realistically. On the other hand the expressions of the sacred characters, ecstatic or devout, tend to be somewhat stylized and in several instances we see that enigmatic smile characteristic of the School of Leonardo.

Attempts have been made to determine the respective shares of the two painters in this huge picture-sequence, by referring to paintings made by them after they had parted company (in 1511); by Yañez in the Cathedral of Cuenca, and by Llanos at Jativa and in Murcia. Also, by seeking to discover which of the two is the more 'Leonardesque', it has been hoped to decide which of them was Leonardo's pupil. This, indeed has been alleged of each of them in turn and on equally plausible grounds. All that can be said for certain is that both painters took much from Leonardo, but were influenced as well by other Italians, notably (as Maria Luisa Caterla has pointed out) by Giorgione in his first period. Yañez is, perhaps, the more vigorous of the two, his art is racy of the soil and naturalistic; Llanos' drawing is less virile. But we find dissimilarities in the output of each of these two men, taken separately; some works obviously owing much to Leonardo, others less. As for the doors of the High Altar, we should certainly be doing Llanos an injustice if we ascribed to him all the weaker scenes, to the exclusion of the others. Actually we have here a joint work whose composition throughout is of a high order and which conveys a strikingly monumental effect, and it reflects much credit on both artists that they could cope so successfully with surfaces of such vast extent. For the value of the whole is not impaired by the differences of quality in the various scenes; moreover, these differences may be partly due to the fact that the scenes on the outside of the doors (which are generally closed) are more exposed than those on the inside. In both cases, however, they are in fairly good condition and the colors (unlike those of most paintings in the style of Leonardo) have kept their luster—which says much for the simple but efficient craftsmanship of the Spanish painters of this period.

As was to be expected, this gigantic work, exhibiting to such effect the 'new style' inspired by Antiquity, in one of the most famous edifices of the Middle Ages, could not fail deeply to impress the artists of the day. There is no question that Juan Vicente Masip, first of a family that produced a great number of painters, belonged to the group of artists who took their lead from the Hernandos. Juan Masip's work was for a long while confused with that of his son, who bore the same name at first but subsequently rose to fame under the name of 'Juan de Juanes.' Though father and son worked together for many years, we see the father's hand alone in a series of works antecedent to their collaboration.

Masip was living at Valencia in 1513 and, as observed above, in touch with the Hernandos; all the same the influence predominating in his art is clearly Raphael's. This is particularly evident in two small panels at the Prado: *The Martyrdom of St Ines* and *The Visitation*. It seems almost certain that Masip spent some time in Italy, but there is no direct proof of this. In his work we find a feeling for volumes, a mastery of the three dimensions and of movement, combined with a sureness of touch, that rank him high amongst the artists of his day.

We find the same qualities, but weakened, cloyed with a sentimental Mannerism, in Juan de Juanes' work which, however, with its vast appeal to the pious instincts of the Spanish populace, won him great celebrity. Italian influences seem to have come to him at second hand and to have lost much of their native vigor in transmission. All the same

JUAN DE JUANES (CA. 1523-1579). THE LAST SUPPER, DETAIL. CHURCH OF SAN NICOLAS, VALENCIA.

the painter has surrendered to them, blindly. His rare efforts to break free and achieve a certain realism—as in the Scenes of the *Martyrdom of St Stephen* (Prado) whose animation is all too obviously theatrical—must be written down as failures. His best works are those which, while following Italian models, have a special note of tenderness and a tang of provincialism not devoid of charm: such as *The Mystical Marriage of the Venerable Agnesio* (Museum of Valencia), his masterwork, and the pictures in the Church of San Nicolás, one of which, *The Last Supper*, has some excellent still-life passages, while the composition is of considerable interest in view of the large part played in it by the tablecloth.

Juanes continued working, but without showing much advance in the quality of his art, until his death, in 1579. He had three children, all painters: Vicente, Dorotea and Margarita. In the work of Margarita especially we see something of the somber violence of her grandfather's art.

Raphael's influence made itself felt in Seville too, but later. Luis de Vergas spent several years in Italy copying Raphael, Correggio and Sebastiano del Piombo before returning to Spain to make (in 1555) an altarpiece, *The Adoration of the Shepherds*, for the Cathedral of Seville. In 1561 he painted the altarpiece oddly named *"La Gamba"* ("the leg") in tribute to the academically flawless drawing of one of Adam's legs. Another artist who worked for a long period in Italy before returning to his native city was the Cordovan Pablo de Cespedes, who stayed abroad for twenty years. An architect, a man of learning and a poet, he was much looked up to by the young artists of his day, especially by Pacheco. But it is obvious that at the end of the 16th century the art of Seville had lost touch with the native impulses of Spanish painting and entered on a path which could lead only to sterile academicism. Indeed the only signs of any vigorous life in Sevillian painting are to be found in the work of foreigners, notably the Flemish artist Pieter de Kempeneer (in Spanish, Pedro de Campaña), who made some excellent portraits. More specifically Dutch influences are discernible in the art of Sturm of Zieriksee. At Valencia the Zarineña family of painters, best of whom was Juan, painted in the Great Hall of the Cortes (in the Palace of the Ayuntamiento) a series of frescos portraying the various Orders of the Assembly: Nobility, Clergy, etc.; these large-scale group compositions remind us both of the Dutch corporation portraits and Venetian groups of Senators in conclave.

Based on a cult of beauty at once ideal and rational, Pacheco's religious works may be regarded as a last reflection of Renaissance art, drained, however, of its content and slightly 'out of true' like scenes reflected in a series of mirrors. Our interest in Pacheco today stems from the fact that he transmitted his vast knowledge of classical and Italian art to Velazquez, his pupil and son-in-law who, while drawing benefit from it, did not permit it to cramp the evolution of his personal genius. Pacheco was far from a mere pedant; while keenly interested in ideas and theories, he kept an observant eye on what was going on around him. This is evidenced both by his "true portraits" of illustrious men (done in red and black crayons) and by his treatise: *Arte de la pintura: su antigüedad y grandeza* (1649), containing *inter alia* biographies of contemporary artists. In it he describes his meeting with El Greco at Toledo in 1611; though startled, indeed shocked by the works he saw and the remarks made by El Greco, he was broad-minded enough to rank the painter among the great masters. The hundred and seventy drawings in his sketch-book, chiefly of ecclesiastics, but also of painters, musicians and military men of his day were made at various dates during his long career, and in them he brings out the characters of his sitters with vivacity and forthrightness.

It should also be observed, and this holds good for the official portraitists of the Court of Philip II, Sanchez Coello and Pantoja de la Cruz, that in the human model these painters found the only outlet available for escaping from 'Roman' classicism into freer air. True, in the lay-out of their portraits they kept to the rules and 'just proportions' they had learnt, yet even within these narrow limits the power of life made itself felt insistently. On the other hand, when dealing with conventional religious or historical subjects, these painters lacked as yet the gift of breathing life into the dry bones of classicism by reintroducing elements of reality.

MORALES AND MANNERISM

In Mannerism we witness an attempt to humanize Classicism by introducing an emotional element into the actual making of the picture. Juan de Juanes had already gone some way in that direction, but he never lost a feeling (inherited from Masip) for architecturally ordered composition in which forms are clearly stated and not allowed to dissolve into their context. Thus Juanes' art may be regarded as a half-way house between Italian Classicism and the realistic Spanish School.

In the art of Luis Morales, on the other hand, the expression of emotion overruled all else; lines merge into each other and even colors acquire a subjective value. We have here a thorough-going Mannerism, unique in Spanish painting. Unfortunately, in his attempts to render mystical exaltation or ecstasy (and he aimed at nothing short of this), Morales had at his disposal only a limited range of means of expression, and these of a somewhat conventional order. True, by ringing the changes on a small number of themes, he succeeded in creating certain stock figures that strongly appealed to the masses. But, unless there is a monumental quality in the subject itself (as in the *Pietà* in the San Fernando Academy), his pictures are submerged in sentimental details, which he often stresses to an unconscionable degree. Now and then he attains a limited perfection, but it is seldom that his initial concept is not whittled down in the process of realization.

All Morales' attempts to treat elaborate themes fail egregiously; movement degenerates into gesticulation, expressions are exaggerated beyond all measure. Whenever he ventures on relatively large compositions, we find huge gaps in them. It is a pity that Morales did not make more portraits; such contacts with reality would have enabled him to palliate his lack of creative imagination. His portrayal of *The Blessed Juan de Ribera* (at the Prado), with its simple, unsophisticated piety, strikes a note of truth rare in his other works.

Philip II invited Morales to Madrid to paint a 'trial picture' for the Escorial, but it did not meet with the royal approval. This decision of the King's may well strike us as much more justifiable than his similar rejection of El Greco; we can hardly imagine any work by Morales coming up to the exacting standard set for the Escorial (so exacting, indeed, that it remained practically empty). Generally speaking, the composition of his pictures is not vigorous enough for them to hold their own in a vast architectural setting and amongst other works; they are at their best when of small dimensions and seen in isolation.

The view of Morales' *œuvre* as a sort of counterpart, admittedly less felicitous, of El Greco's seems to set too high a value on it. No doubt both painters had a way of using the same theme again and again, but Morales did this with a view to deepening an emotion, refining on it more and more, whereas El Greco gives us a series of variations, employing so rich a counterpoint that the initial theme loses its importance and serves as a mere point of departure. And though Morales, too, indulges in distortions in his renderings of bodies and faces, these are not conditioned, as with El Greco, by the inner life of forms but serve as easily recognizable expressive signs—a rudimentary 'language of the heart'.

His cold, thin colors impart a vague melancholy, not devoid of charm, to all his work, and some have seen in this a consequence of the painter's humble origin (he hailed from Badajoz, a town in the poverty-stricken province of Estremadura, and spent his whole life there) and also of his contacts with the Portuguese Schools in his formative years. Lafuente Ferrari regards Morales' work as an attempt to stem the main historical current of Spanish art during this period. But it is probable that this seeming 'resistance' was due rather to an inner conflict in the artist's temperament than to a response to the harsh, austere conditions of life in rural Spain throughout her history. Morales was beloved by his contemporaries, who called him '*El divino*'. Today, however, we see in his works only a specious appearance of faith, sensibility and sweetness, without any solid qualities behind it. Indeed it might be called un-Spanish, for the essence of Spanish art is a very real feeling for the raw material, so to speak, of life and a gift of peopling even its most otherworldly creations with truly living presences.

THE COURT PAINTERS OF PHILIP II

As against Morales whose life was spent in sadness and seclusion, the 'Courtier Painter' as we might describe him, Sanchez Coello, cuts the figure of a happy man and, as an artist, one of fortune's favorites. With the accession of Philip II the Spanish Court, now permanently in residence in the palaces of Madrid and its environs, and about to find in the Escorial a symbolical expression of that unbending dignity on which the monarch set such store, became a self-contained, well-organized entity which drew to itself all that was most active in the life of Spain and incarnated with a somber brilliance (if sometimes with a somewhat ludicrous insouciance) the aspirations and virtues of the Spanish race. Though this stately fabric had a curious rigidity, it exercised a vast fascination on all who were invited to co-operate. For the King never flagged in his efforts to give Imperial Spain an artistic décor worthy of her greatness. His father had left him a superb collection of works by the great Venetians, Titian, Tintoretto and Veronese, which had made an indelible impression on his artistic taste. He was acquainted with Dutch art, too, particularly relishing Patinir and Hieronymus Bosch. But though in the Escorial, whose plans he himself had drawn up and whose building he personally supervised, he achieved an admirable fusion between the monumental classical style and the most typically Spanish setting, he was not so fortunate with his painters. The Venetian masters whom he invited to Madrid turned a deaf ear to the royal summons and he had qualms about employing El Greco, their obvious successor. He was happily inspired when his choice fell on Juan Fernandez de Navarrete, known as El Mudo because at an early age he had lost the power of speech. Born in 1526 at Logroño, this painter perhaps had studied in Italy, under Titian. In such of his works as have survived (unfortunately relatively few and in bad condition) we find a grave, rather somber naturalism and an intimate feeling for his models combined with a taste, rare at the time, for realistic detail. Stripping religious subjects of all emphasis and the pompous trappings of classicism, Navarrete replaces these by scenes of everyday life, and though these scenes are somewhat bleak, impersonal and frigid, he does his best to animate them by bold experiments in light effects; indeed there is hardly any extant work by him in which he fails to approach the problems of space, light and compositional structure from an original angle. In an unfinished picture, *The Burial of St Lawrence* (1579), a figure in the foreground is illuminated by a candle he holds partly screened behind his hand and in the clashes of vivid light with darkness we have a striking anticipation of the 'Tenebrism' practised by Caravaggio a few years later. To Navarrete was entrusted the important task of painting the altars of the Escorial Church, but he was unable to carry it through. By his premature death in 1579 (at Toledo) Spain lost an artist who might well have enabled Spanish art to strike out on its destined path at an earlier date. Its immediate result was that a group of rather bombastic and mediocre Italian painters, Luca Cambiaso, Federico Zuccaro and Peregrino Tibaldi, were called in to continue the work, seconded by some second-rank Spanish artists the best of whom was Luis de Carvajal. Sanchez Coello, too, was invited to complete the work begun by Navarrete; he did this in the 'Roman' style at its most frigid and conventional, in fact it seemed that his great predecessor's innovations were for him a dead letter.

All the same Sanchez Coello was a great painter, though not in this field. It was in his portraits that he proved himself a pioneer. Was Philip II aware, while he was trying to force the hand of destiny and to endow Spain with huge decorative paintings vying with those of Italy, that under his auspices the beginnings of a revolution in the world of art were taking form: a revolution that was to make its effect felt when, with a growing comprehension and respect of Man and a deeper insight into the humblest secrets of the visible world (even though that world were limited to the Royal Court) a whole new realm of art was to come into being under Velazquez' triumphant brush? To Sanchez Coello falls the credit of having prepared the way for this triumph, though we must not overlook his debt to the artist who was his teacher and initiator, that famous Dutchman Anton van Moor, known in Spain as Antonio Moro and in England as Sir Anthony More.

ALONSO SANCHEZ COELLO (1531/32-1588).
PORTRAIT OF PHILIP II (CA. 1575). (34½×28¼")
PRADO, MADRID.

Thoroughly Italianate in his handling of forms (with Mannerism and Romanism in the ascendant), but spiritually a man of the Atlantic coast, and endowed both with an almost mystical insight and a fearless love of truth, Coello is a striking case of cosmopolitanism at its best and most rewarding. Born near Valencia and coming of a noble Spanish family who had long devoted themselves to the service of the Crown of Portugal, he was educated in Lisbon in a refined and cultivated milieu and inured at an early age to the discipline of classical studies. Impressed by the boy's intelligence, Moro spared no pains in shaping his talent and in the course of time Coello inherited Moro's high position in the favor of the King, who even addressed him as "my very dear son." Though an accomplished courtier, basking in the friendship of princes and grandees, Coello did not palter with the truth. His portraits combine precision and finesse, not to say preciosity, with shrewd observation of his sitters, all the more effective for its seeming nonchalance. The painter stood back from his model, observed him with detachment and punctilious reserve—which was perhaps the best method of approach since it did not rouse suspicion and the painter could explore, unawares, the secret places of his heart. One of his most famous works shows us the lovely Princess of Eboli with a black bandage over her blind eye; and such is the painter's skill that this incongruity does not jar on us in the least. Indeed Coello inaugurated what was nothing short of a new school of court portraiture; his immediate successor was Pantoja de la Cruz who, though no great hand at religious subjects, was like Coello a remarkably fine portraitist; and this tradition of Spanish portrait-painting continued without a break up to Velazquez.

FRANCISCO RIBALTA

But, for the noble art of Velazquez to arise, Spanish painting had first to recover its unity. To Francisco Ribalta is due the credit of having succeeded in reconciling its various trends and assimilating what was best in the new developments, tentative as yet and unco-ordinated. While justly regarded as the 'patriarch' of the classical Spanish school, he was essentially a man of the 16th century. He was born shortly after 1550 at Castellon, that is to say at the point of junction between Catalonia and the East, but it would seem that his talent was given its direction at Valencia where he came in contact with the work of Juan de Juanes and with the man himself, though even now he showed signs of rebelling against the conventions of Juanes' Mannerism. It was probably in Madrid rather than in the course of an (unproved) stay in Italy that he became acquainted with the recent develop-ments of Italian art. As a young painter he took much the same standpoint (though more firmly and with surer taste) as that of Navarrete el Mudo, who was then in full possession of his powers and obviously had much influence on him. Nevertheless Ribalta's personality asserted itself from the start with a quiet confidence that led him to press Navarrete's naturalistic and luminist procedures to their logical conclusion. Tormo has pointed out, and quite rightly, that the sources of Ribalta's naturalism were exclusively Spanish. Indeed he seems to have deliberately shunned the cosmopolitan atmosphere of the Court and it was at Valencia, to which city he returned at the close of the century, that he turned out his best work. He led a very active life at Valencia, where he founded a College of Painters and an influential school. Meanwhile he made large *ensembles* for the College of the Patriarchate, the Church of Algemesi and the Carthusian monastery of Portacoeli, and it is from what survives of these large-scale works that we learn how great an artist he actually was. For he gave Spain nothing short of a new style and, like Caravaggio in Italy, broke with the classical Italian formalism which hitherto had reigned supreme. No longer idealizing forms, he applied himself to restoring to them truth and plenitude by a highly expert handling of chiaroscuro and the exaltation of volumes flooded with light. His vigorous drawing owes much to a thorough knowledge of anatomy and even his most elaborate compositions are adjusted to the scale of the real world. Thus after a slow and sometimes disappointing evolution, the Spanish Renaissance culminated in an achievement worthy of the splendid promise of its dawn—a new awareness of Man and his place in the scheme of things.

FRANCISCO RIBALTA (1551 OR 1555-1628). SAN BRUNO. FROM THE PORTACOELI RETABLE.
SAN CARLOS MUSEUM, VALENCIA.

EL GRECO

While deriving in its inception from Byzantine and oriental traditions, El Greco's art brought to Spain all that was best in the artistic culture of sixteenth-century Italy. But his genius attained its fullest and most original expression only when it had been permeated by the atmosphere of Spain and, especially, by that of Toledo. Hence the interesting fact that his art provides a sort of résumé of the whole history of primitive Spanish painting which, starting out from the same premises and drawing nourishment from the same sources, displays a progressive transfiguration of themes and technical procedures. The following chapter sets forth the successive stages by which the painter, now a Spaniard, achieved his honored place amongst the greatest creative spirits that the world has known. In the forefront of our second volume will be shown the contribution made by El Greco to the delineation of the social order of his day, that world at once erudite, chivalrous and profoundly religious of the Spanish "Golden Age", of which The Burial of Count Orgaz *is a glorious and perdurable memorial.*

EL GRECO (1541-1614). THE VIRGIN MARY. DETAIL FROM THE HOLY FAMILY (CA. 1585).
HOSPITAL OF TAVERA, TOLEDO.

EL GRECO (1541-1614). THE HOLY SPIRIT. DETAIL FROM THE TRINITY (1577).
PRADO, MADRID.

EL GRECO

CURIOUSLY enough, the first world-famous name in Spanish painting is not a Spanish name at all, but the half-Italian appellation given a foreigner who, while never greatly troubling to adjust his way of living to the Spanish pattern, made authentically his own the spirit of Spain. In the history of art there are other examples of great artists' identifying themselves with an adopted country—an assimilation natural enough when we consider the, so to speak, universalism on a lofty plane to which art points the way; but rarely have such assimilations taken so dramatic a form.

On official documents in which he had to specify his age and place of origin El Greco stated that he was a "Candiot," a rather indefinite term since during that period it was often used by extension to mean 'Cretan,' and not necessarily an inhabitant of Candia, the capital of the island. Such evidence as there is, however, points to the fact that Candia was actually his birthplace and the alternative theory which has been advanced, that he was born at Fodele, a village near Candia, has little to support it.

At that time Crete still formed part of the Venetian Empire; it was not seriously threatened by the Turks until a century later and succumbed to them only in 1669. The population of the island, which was then considerable, comprised Catholic Venetians as well as Greeks, mostly of the Orthodox persuasion. El Greco came of a well-to-do and highly esteemed family which, it would seem, had emigrated to Crete from Byzantium, after a halt *en route* at Corfu. As a boy, he was given a sound classical education, strongly marked by the scientific trend of Italian humanism at this time. He would seem to have remained a Catholic throughout his life.

A school of Byzantine painting flourished in Crete, rivaling that of Macedonia and adhering to the art tradition of the monks of Mount Athos, though already impregnated with Venetian influences, and it was doubtless in one of the studios working in contact with the local monasteries that El Greco learned the art of painting.

There are many reminiscences of Byzantine art in El Greco's *œuvre*, and they persist right up to the end of his career; indeed, curiously enough, they seem to gather strength and intensity with the passing of the years and the lengthening of the gap between him and his Cretan upbringing. All the same they are always sporadic and incidental and though their importance on the technical as well as on the spiritual plane is not to be denied, they hardly justify so categorical a view as that taken, to begin with, by A.L. Mayer (but subsequently retracted by him): that El Greco must not be regarded as a Spanish painter or as belonging to the Spanish school. Fairly close affinities have been detected between certain details, generally of a minor and unobtrusive order (such as the angel in *The Tears of St Peter* or the scene of the Stoning of St Stephen in *The Burial of Count Orgaz*), and the work of El Greco's compatriot Michael Damascenos (or Damaskinos), which includes the icons of an uncompromisingly Byzantine pattern in Candia Cathedral and the murals in the church known as St George of the Greeks at Venice. Certain highly elaborate compositions such as that of the *Supper in the House of Simon* have analogies in the output of Damascenos; thus the placing of figures at the extremities of a long rectangle that we find in *Pentecost* is typically Byzantine, and the almond-shaped faces in, for example, *The Coronation of the Virgin* are in the tradition of the East.

On the technical side, El Greco kept to the Byzantine practice of beginning by covering the entire picture surface with a uniform ground, ochre, white, black or green as the case might be, and drawing on it lines subdividing the picture into sections, then painting each part successively and waiting for each coat of paint to dry before continuing. This explains why so many 'works in progress' were always to be seen in his studio—those "brutal sketches" which shocked Pacheco so much when he visited the painter. El Greco painted both in oils and in tempera, the medium always used by the Byzantines. Finally, Byzantine procedures are manifest in El Greco's arbitrarily foreshortened perspectives, the lack of depth in his pictures, his practice of posting close up in the foreground, in front of a very low horizon, figures that wear a strangely visionary air, like phantoms from another world.

None the less there is a world of difference between El Greco's methods and the conventional rigidity of Byzantine art. With El Greco all is movement, impassioned exaltation, a flux of living forms in constant evolution. Here we have, no doubt, what he acquired from Italy. Moreover, his figures, though bathed in an ideal light and embodying deep religious feeling, states of ecstasy and celestial visions, are never mere abstractions. They participate in the world of flesh and blood, even in its crudest manifestations and, as Maurice Barrès put it, express "orgasms of the soul." In fact we find in them a curious blend of spirituality and sensuality. And this, no doubt, is what he acquired from Spain.

This constant transformation of the basic elements of Byzantinism, their adaptation to Italian forms and to a more complex and advanced psychology, suggests that El Greco migrated to Venice when still quite young, probably in or about 1560. Not only the capital *par excellence* of arts and letters, Venice was also the political capital of the Cretans. A large Greek colony numbering over four thousand persons lived and prospered around the canal named for this reason the Rio dei Greci, the focal point of the colony being St George's Church. Greek artists and artisans, whose work was highly esteemed by the Venetians, were so numerous that they had a Guild of their own. It was in this Greco-Italian climate that El Greco's genius came into its own and his art acquired that fertile dualism of East and West which enabled him to benefit by his contacts with the Venetian painters.

There is a very old tradition that El Greco was a pupil of Titian. Now that a fair number of his earliest works have been identified, it would seem that he began by frequenting the *bottega* of Jacopo Bassano, whose solid naturalism smacking of the soil he imitated rather awkwardly, but from whose 'luminist' experiments he derived more benefit.

EL GRECO (1541-1614). THE CARPENTER. DETAIL FROM THE ESPOLIO (1579).
CATHEDRAL OF TOLEDO.

EL GRECO (1541-1614). PORTRAIT OF JULIÁN ROMERO DE LAS AZANAS,
DETAIL (1580-1585). PRADO, MADRID.

It would seem that in 1565 and 1566 he underwent the one truly decisive influence of his career: that of Tintoretto, whose passionate temperament was so obviously akin to his own. From Tintoretto he learnt the art of grouping figures, making them come to life in architectural settings adjusted to an appropriate rhythm, and moving them freely in space without regard to normal visual perspective. It is known that throughout his career El Greco had the habit, like Tintoretto, of making models in wax or wood of the figures he was about to paint—which enabled him to move those figures at will within a given setting. He acquired something, too, from Veronese: a predilection for fully modeled figures, rich textures and particular colors, notably green. Finally, Titian, with whom El Greco worked between 1567 and 1569, imparted to him that amazing mastery of the brushstroke which characterizes Titian's last phase. The favorite painter of the Emperor Charles V and Philip II was then in extreme old age and had developed his technique in the direction of a sort of Impressionism capable of expressing the subtlest atmospheric nuances. It was from Titian that El Greco probably learnt to concentrate on general effect, even at the cost of 'finish.'

El Greco's early works show very diverse tendencies; he was obviously casting about for his destined path. Some, the more elaborate works, show that he had quickly mastered the Venetian procedures: deep structural recession, richly modeled forms, fluent movements. These works, which have affinities with those of Veronese and even those of Correggio (whose pictures he copied), illustrate an important stage in his development, but one that left no lasting mark. Examples are *The Adoration of the Shepherds* (Bergamo) and the two versions of *The Healing of the Blind Man* (Dresden and Parma); and if these were all El Greco's work we had, we should write him down as a good second-rank Venetian painter. But there are other works, sometimes more archaic and sketch-like, which come nearer the pictures he was to paint in Spain; they link up the painter's Cretan beginnings with his ultimate achievement. Thus the remarkable polyptych at Modena (discovered and discussed by Pallucchini) includes themes so thoroughly Byzantine that some have thought El Greco must have painted it at Candia and brought it with him to Italy. Against this is the fact that in other scenes, especially an early *Annunciation*, the technique is of a much more developed order.

Nothing better illustrates El Greco's keen interest in the masterworks of his time than his magnificent drawing after Michelangelo's *Day*, the unfinished version of which was sold in 1563 at Venice by an antiquary. Besides an admirable rendering of the volumes, the painter, as we can clearly see, was fascinated by the ascending movement imparted to all the forms. Thus it is not surprising that, after absorbing all that Venice had to teach him, he decided to move to Rome in quest of fresh fields of artistic experience. On his way he stopped at Parma and Reggio (where he copied Correggio's *Night* in a very characteristic manner) and perhaps at Florence, too.

The Roman art-world, over which the academic heirs of Raphael, devotees of an eclectic Mannerism, held undisputed sway, must have been all the less congenial to El Greco in that, already conscious of his great gifts, he dreamed of measuring himself against the Masters on an equal footing. Probably his departure from Venice was due to an unconscious craving both for a change of atmosphere and a spell of solitude in which he could take stock of, and develop, his resources. Thus Renaissance Rome, with its pomps and vanities, meant for him but a temporary halting-place in his spiritual pilgrimage. He came to Rome, it seems, in 1569. The well-known letter of Giulio Clovio, an eminent miniature-painter who though of Croatian extraction was known as 'The Macedonian,' is dated 1570. In this letter he commended to Cardinal Farnese a young Cretan, Titian's pupil, who was worthy to rank beside the greatest painters of the day and had already created much stir among the Roman artists with a quite remarkable self-portrait. El Greco's brief stay at the Palazzo Farnese is noteworthy chiefly for the contacts he made with painters and writers frequenting it, and especially for the friendships he struck up (through the instrumentality of the librarian Fulvio Orsini) with several Spanish humanists, one of whom was Luis de Castilla, a Toledan, brother of the dean of the Primatical Cathedral. An interesting letter (discovered in Croatia) is extant, in which Clovio describes a visit he paid to El Greco one spring day when everyone was out in the streets of Rome, enjoying the sunshine. The curtains were closely drawn and the painter was seated in his darkened studio, neither working nor sleeping. "He refused to come out with me," Clovio continues, "explaining that the light of day impaired his inner light."

We hear of the reasons why El Greco was obliged to leave Rome in or about 1572 from an entry in the Memoirs of Cesare Mancini, physician to Pope Urban VIII, written forty years later, and thus at second-hand. When there was talk of draping the nudes in Michelangelo's *Last Judgment* El Greco declared that if the whole work was torn down he could remake it in a decent, seemly manner, and of a quality equal to that of the original. So infuriated were the disciples and admirers of Michelangelo by this remark that he was forced to leave the city. A sketch for a *Last Judgment*, found and published by Hugo Kehrer in 1940, is perhaps a relic of El Greco's project. After all this reaction on the part of the Roman art-world was only to be expected; a whole school of artists was thriving on reminiscences and ever feebler imitations of the work of Raphael and Michelangelo, and their whole *raison d'être* was imperiled by this outrageous proposal.

Though El Greco greatly admired Michelangelo's sculpture his dislike of the great Italian's painting was inveterate—he reiterated it in his old age when Pacheco came to see him—and due to a fundamental difference of views. He was all against such attempts to bring down celestial visions to the level of terrestrial scenes, however grandiose their presentation. To his mind, the forms of classical antiquity were wholly unsuited for sacred subjects and Christian faith could but be sullied by contacts with the mythology of the pagan past. For the same reason he was against any sort of 'naturalism' in the renderings of such themes. This view was shared by many religious-minded men of the day. "What mystical emotion can we experience when we see a naked Christ?" asked Ludovico Dolce (quoted by Pacheco). In this respect El Greco may be regarded as a last embodiment of the mediaeval spirit, bringing a great period to a triumphant close; in all other respects, however, he opened windows on a new world and pointed the way to modern art.

All the same El Greco took over much from Roman Mannerism: his iconography, his practice of representing sacred figures under an idealized, less and less individualized aspect (the exact opposite of the procedure followed by the Primitives), his oval or circular composition with the expressive elements in the center, the anecdotal and more realistic details being relegated to the circumference. He found that this arrangement was more suitable than the horizontal, always somewhat theatrical, lay-outs of Venetian art, for conjuring up heavenly visions and spiritual ecstasies. No longer earthbound, forms are swept upwards in a vast ascending movement; garments become mere planes of color, subject to rhythms on which gravity has no effect, and participating in the life of the divine or human figure they envelop—a procedure which, centuries later, was not to be lost on Cézanne. After noting what El Greco took from Parmigianino, Pontormo and even Zuccaro, Lionello Venturi remarks that at Rome he learnt the expressive value of bizarre forms, as at Venice that of color. The German authorities Dvorak and Kehrer see in El Greco the last great European Mannerist, the man of genius who at last fulfilled the dream of so many artists, of creating truly celestial light.

Portraits bulk large in El Greco's output during his stay in Rome, amongst them those of Giulio Clovio (Naples Museum) and Vincentio Anastagi. In *Christ Driving the Traders from the Temple*, he depicts a group of persons who were the gods of the art-world of the day: Titian, Michelangelo, Giulio Clovio and (though this identification is not so certain) Raphael. To this period may probably be assigned the early versions of the *Espolio*, his first masterpiece in Spain. Thus in 1572 when he left Rome he was in full possession of his *métier*, and all that was needed for his conceptions to blossom forth in concrete form was a favorable soil.

It is only four years later that we definitely learn of El Greco's being in Spain. What was he doing in the interval? There is no satisfactory proof of the theory that he went straight to Madrid and took part in some of the minor decorative or architectural work in progress at the Escorial. He may have halted in Malta where some traces of his presence

EL GRECO (1541-1614). CHRIST ON THE CROSS (1590-1595). (69¾×42½")
ZULOAGA MUSEUM, ZUMAYA.

EL GRECO (1541-1614). THE VIRGIN MARY. DETAIL FROM THE CRUCIFIXION (1590-1595).
PRADO, MADRID.

EL GRECO (1541-1614). ST JOHN. DETAIL FROM THE CRUCIFIXION (1590-1595).
PRADO, MADRID.

EL GRECO (1541-1614). THE TEARS OF ST PETER (1590-1595). (44×41¼″)
HOSPITAL OF TAVERA, TOLEDO.

are still extant. Though it was at Toledo (in 1577) that he was given his first large-scale
order, when he was commissioned, by the good offices of Diego de Castilla, dean of the
Cathedral Chapter, to make the altarpiece of Santo Domingo el Antiguo, we can deduce

from certain clauses in the contract that he was working in Madrid at the time. He was already living with Doña Jeronima de las Cuevas who was to be his life's companion. He had brought to Madrid some pictures painted in Italy and his reputation was evidently well-established, the contract specifying that the entire work was to be done by his hand.

During his residence in Madrid El Greco certainly came in contact with the artists employed at the Escorial; amongst them were a great many Italians, including the sculptor Pompeo Leoni, a personal friend of his, and one of the Spaniards was Navarrete el Mudo who, like El Greco, was said to have studied under Titian. Obviously El Greco was interested in Navarrete's work, for he adopted certain features of his iconography, notably in his renderings of saints. But El Greco was far too conscious of his powers (of which he made no secret when he came to Toledo) to be willing to take a share in minor works. To this period may be ascribed his big composition *The Adoration of the Name of Jesus*, subsequently mistitled *The Dream of King Philip II*. The execution of this work, in which the special use of colors, the golden light put on in small, excited brushstrokes, the incisive drawing, and the still typically Venetian modeling suggest a transitional art astride between Italy and Spain, justifies us in agreeing with Camon Aznar as to its date, 1576 or 1577. The view put forward by some that this picture was made later, after the death of Philip II, has no serious backing. Indeed it is far more probable that this was meant to be the 'trial picture' required from all who wished to take part in the decoration of the Escorial.

Remembering perhaps his ambitious project of painting a new *Last Judgment* for the Sistine Chapel, El Greco seems to have crowded into this picture all possible proofs of his skill in composition and amazing technical proficiency. Drawing his inspiration from St Paul, he depicts heaven, earth and hell adoring the name of Jesus. The presentation of the three worlds is highly original and El Greco still employs a somewhat deep perspective; hell is represented at the edge of the terrestrial world, its approach being through the gaping mouth of a monster (a Byzantine motif). There is no distortion of the figures. But the backgrounds are very summarily indicated—almost as if this were the preliminary draft of a more elaborate composition.

In the summer of 1577 El Greco went to Toledo to work on the Santo Domingo altarpiece, and the enlightened understanding of his work shown by the Toledans, their obvious admiration (vouched for by a steady flow of commissions), and also no doubt the affinities he felt with this unique city, built on a rock whose ruggedness reminded him of his homeland, with its mixed population of converted Jews, Moors and foreigners of all descriptions —all these, we may be sure, were factors in his decision to settle in Toledo. Thus the great traveler always eager for new experience, the wanderer ever in quest of kindred souls to understand him, found at last his journey's end, and asked for nothing better than to feast his eyes day after day on those wooded, stony hillsides concealing marvellous gardens, and on the mirroring waters of the Tagus spangled with sudden glints of color. For the thirty-six creative years which lay before him, this great Cretan expatriate was to find in Toledo the home of his election.

In 1578 a son was born to him, Jorge Manuel, who later worked in close association with him. We know very little of his homelife except that it was a happy one. The problem of Doña Jeronima's position remains unsolved; no proof that he was married to her has been forthcoming, nor is she ever referred to as the mother of his son. It has been argued that the marriage must certainly have taken place, in view of the improbability that, considering the period and the *milieu*, such an irregular union could have been tolerated in the case of a painter patronized so lavishly by the Church. One may wonder, however, if the nineteenth century did not take a slightly warped view of the conditions of social life in earlier centuries; strict as these may have been in Spain under the iron rule of Philip II and the Inquisition, it was not till somewhat later that a rigorous morality prevailed. Nor must we forget the sort of place that sixteenth-century Toledo was: a melting-pot of different races, religions and traditions, and we may surmise that many anomalies and unconventional modes of living managed to survive, if in discreet reclusion, under the colorful surface of

Toledan life. Camon Aznar, who advocates the theory of a marriage between Jeronima and the painter, has very rightly pointed out that, contrary to the view endorsed by Barrès that El Greco's art expresses the profound melancholy of a once great city in its decline, the city by the Tagus was enjoying much prosperity when El Greco settled there. Toledo's decline, a very rapid one, began only with the opening years of the 17th century, the years when the painter, now at an advanced age, had retired from public life and was devoting himself to research-work on his own account. The departure of the Court, whose residence at Toledo had always been intermittent, had no influence on the prosperity of the city in 1561. It was still famed throughout Europe for its silk, weaving, brocades, ceramics (the famous *azulejos* of Talavera) and especially its sword-blades. The death-blow was dealt these industries only in 1609-10, with the King's decree for the expulsion of the Moors.

Toledo was—and still is—the ecclesiastic capital of Spain: which meant in those days the presence of a fabulous hoard of treasures and a vast number of churches, convents, colleges and foundations. It was while El Greco was living there that the great Church of St John the Baptist and the Hospital of Tavera (so huge a building that in painting his *View of Toledo* El Greco had to shift it from its real site so as not to obscure the panorama of the city) were brought to completion. Also the Chapel of the Sagrario and the Mozarabic Chapel on which Jorge Manuel worked were added to the Cathedral during this period. New convents were built, and much work was done on the Ayuntamiento and the Alcazar.

Toledo was, above all, the intellectual and spiritual metropolis; "glory of Spain, light of the arts and Holy City," thus Cervantes (who lived there for some time) described it, and he made it the setting of two of his *Novelas Exemplares*. The greatest mystics of the century, St Teresa and St John of the Cross, left their mark there. With its twenty-two eminent professors, Toledo University, then at the height of its renown, could vie with the greatest universities of the Catholic world, Salamanca and Bologna. Writers and men of learning met regularly for friendly discussions of all the problems of the day, the most favored meeting-places being the residences of Count Fuensalida and Count Mora and Cardinal Sandova's country house, the famous 'Cigarral de Buenavista.' Complete freedom of speech was the order of the day at these gatherings; but, however different their views, these men were fervently united in the quest of moral perfection and of beauty. Indeed the atmosphere that prevailed was far more that of the Italian Renaissance than that of the heyday of the Inquisition. El Greco's closest friends were Fray Hortensio Paravicino and the jurist Covarrubias (whose portrait he often painted); also the great poet Góngora, Ercilla, the explorer of Patagonia, and Baltasar Gracian, author of *The Courtier*. In this company of men of wit and culture, the part played by women—the beautiful and proud ladies of Toledo who as Gracian wrote "could say everything with a single word"—must have been all of tact and discreet charm.

Such, we may imagine, was the part played by Doña Jeronima in El Greco's life. It is believed that she was the model for the face of the Virgin, painted with a tenderness and abandon rare in El Greco's art, as she figures in so many of his pictures, loveliest of all being the Virgin in the Tavera *Holy Family*. There is a quiet, very human beauty in the face of this young woman with the melting eyes, finely sensitive nostrils and small, softly modeled mouth; into that realm of sublime, all-but-disincarnate beings which is the sphere of El Greco's religious art, she brings a warmly human presence. Thus we may picture the artist's life as moving, so to speak, on two quite different planes. On one he was the man who is completely happy in his home, if always with a faint nostalgic yearning for his island birthplace. Thus he had his elder brother, Manusso, come to live with him (we see his face in several portraits: the fur-wrapped face of an old man with an otherworldly air), and it was in Toledo that Manusso died. Also El Greco gave a ready welcome to the Greek travelers who came to collect funds for the ransom of some relation held captive by the Infidels. On the other plane he was the great artist, erudite and a dreamer of strange dreams, who had succeeded in giving visible form to the most purely mystical conceptions, and whose opinions on art's eternal problems were eagerly sought after by contemporaries.

EL GRECO (1541-1614) THE CORONATION OF THE VIRGIN (1595-1600). (35½×39¼″)
PRADO, MADRID.

The inventory of his library, made after his death, shows how wide were his interests, ranging from Greek tragedy to the sciences and architecture. (As a matter of fact El Greco fancied himself as an architect and wrote a long treatise on this subject; unfortunately no trace of it survives.) Books in Greek included Homer, Euripides, Demosthenes, Isocrates and Aristotle, Lucian and Aesop rubbing shoulders with the Greek Bible and the works of the Fathers of the Church. Amongst his Italian books, besides Petrarch, Tasso and Ariosto, were found two medical treatises; also Vitruvius, Palladio, Alberti, Vignola, compendia of Roman Antiquities, contemporary works by Botero and by Francesco Patrizzi, a writer who boldly declared that Aristotle's philosophy was incompatible with Christian Revelation and that "light is the synthesis and the expression of godhead."

EL GRECO (1541-1614). ST ILDEFONSO WRITING AT THE VIRGIN'S DICTATION (1607). (62×40″)
CHURCH OF THE HOSPITAL OF THE CARIDAD, ILLESCAS.

He had a well-organized studio, in which were employed Francisco Preboste (his servant and factotum, whom he had probably brought with him from Italy), Jorge Manuel, as soon as he was old enough to work as an apprentice, and Luis Tristan. Their task was to ensure a steady supply of versions of the subjects in most demand throughout the Province and beyond its borders. In 1597 Preboste was sent to Seville to collect the sums due from an agent commissioned to sell El Greco's pictures on the local market.

Though the passing years have brought few changes to Toledo, not all El Greco's various residences have been identified. We know, however, that he stayed longest in a group of buildings which had belonged to a nobleman who dabbled in sorcery, the Marquis of Villena, and stood on the site of the mansion of Samuel Levi, the famous Jewish banker of Peter the Cruel, who had him assassinated so as to lay hands on his fortune. Here El Greco rented, at a substantial figure, a suite of rooms extending to the main Palace building. He left them for a time but returned for good in 1604, when he took over no less than twenty-four rooms, not to mention gardens, courtyards and patios. This period marked the high tide of his prosperity, when he lived in conditions of much elegance and luxury; a contemporary tells us that he had musicians in to play to him at his meals. Actually he seems to have been fonder of collecting rare and precious objects than of what we now call comfort and many dealings of his with goldsmiths and embroiderers are on record. None the less the inventory made of his estate after his death on April 7, 1614, shows that he died a poor man. Indeed for some years (mention of that diligent factotum Preboste ceases in 1607) his fortunes had been on the down-grade. His strength had evidently been failing, for he was unable to walk even the short distance to his studio when Pacheco visited him, and he now devoted himself to purely personal experiments in rhythms and pigments, without troubling if his work were saleable. Toledo was now in the throes of a depression, the days of luxurious living were over, poets and art patrons leaving the city. Jorge Manuel, however, kept his father's house and even made some improvements; but the ramshackle, decrepit building could not long survive. In the Museum now installed under the name of El Greco's House, we have but a reconstitution (though much taste and understanding have gone to its making) of what the painter's home must have been. Its site is approximately the same as that of the original house, and from its windows and terraces we have a view over the Tagus and the city of Toledo—the same magnificent view that El Greco had under his eyes day after day.

But the significance of El Greco's life lies in the evolution of his art, its gradual rejection of all carnal attributes in an arduous, unremitting progress towards the eternal. In his first period at Toledo Greco had not forgotten Venice and the Venetian technique: warm tones, broadly modeled forms and balanced composition. But he transmuted these, in terms of his personal vision, into sweeping planes of color, forms moving freely in space, seen from below or from above, their angles rounded off by sudden bursts of light. In the huge altarpiece of Santo Domingo el Antiguo (partly dispersed) we have a fusion of all the most recent tendencies of the painting of the century. *The Ascension* with its tall, tranquil figures reminds us of Titian; in *The Adoration of the Shepherds* distortions of bodies, necessitated by the nocturnal lighting, make their appearance; the figures of the saints have the proportions of Baroque sculpture; while *The Trinity* at the Prado is the most characteristic work. In it the forms have all the massive relief of Michelangelo's, yet they spurn the earth, sublimated by the color symbolism on to a celestial plane. In the sky the dominant colors are white, symbol of godhead, and yellow symbolizing the divine wisdom, source of all light. This work, with all that was best in contemporary Italian art fused together and assimilated in a new, compelling style, came as a revelation. Nothing of the sort had been seen before in Spain and El Greco was promptly hailed as one of the leading painters of the day.

The great *Espolio* in the Cathedral of Toledo is perhaps his most expressionist work. All the accepted rules of composition are waived in deference to the inner exigencies of the subject. Perspective has gone by the board; all we have is a throng of figures surging around Christ, a storm of angry passions which for all its fierceness has no effect on the sad and solitary face of the Divine Victim and seems indeed to swerve away from the huge patch of color made by His red tunic. Only the group of the Holy Women on the left and the joiner at work on the right stand out from the flat surface, forming two masses of strongly indicated volumes. The boldness of the technique in handling certain details, such as the foreshortening of profiles and the light effects on helmets, anticipates the art of Velazquez. To this period belong the artist's most human and most touching portrayals of the face of Christ, bearing the Cross or imprinting his likeness on Veronica's veil. Thus in creating a language to express the spiritual ecstasies of sixteenth-century Spain, El Greco achieved a simplicity foreshadowing the remarkable directness of approach he was to employ at a later phase in his portraits of contemporaries.

It was perhaps because he departed from these principles that he failed in his great venture of 1580 (the trial picture for the Escorial). In his *Martyrdom of St Maurice and the Theban Legion* he tried to speed up the rhythm of his evolution (the subject of the picture and also perhaps the way of handling it was enjoined on him) and crowded so many new procedures into the work that the King was frankly disconcerted. Here as in *The Adoration of the Name of Jesus* the action takes place on three planes. The most important shows a sort of spiritual colloquy in progress between St Maurice and his companions; everything here is conveyed by the attitudes of bodies, gestures of the hands conveying explanation or resignation, and the mystical illumination of the faces. This scene occupies the foreground and the martyrdom itself is shown immediately behind, while the naked forms of the soldiers and victims in the background have the curiously spectral appearance of the forms in the *Adoration*. The heavenly host, waiting to welcome in the martyrs, is showering rays of light upon them. On the dim, unstable soil, beside his signature, in a tangle of wild flowers, El Greco has inserted the stump of a felled tree—perhaps a symbol.

This work failed to please the King; he had it placed in a Sala Capitular, instead of in the church for which it was intended, and commissioned Romulo Cincinnati to make another version of the theme. It was no doubt this setback that prompted El Greco to give his art a new direction; pending that last period when he gave free rein to his bold imaginings, he now tried to fall into line with the Spanish taste for realism and somewhat to reduce the part played by the supernatural. In *The Burial of Count Orgaz* we have the most perfect example of a fusion between the real and the celestial worlds. For the two parts of this famous picture cannot be separated; they complement and explain each other. The saints miraculously appear among the living men, their gorgeous, glittering vestments contrasting with the black garb of the mourners, who betray no surprise at the presence of these heavenly visitants. In the white radiance of the divine light forms are prodigiously elongated, as in the case of St John the Baptist Intercessor who seems to be climbing over the balcony of heaven. We shall deal later with this great work, which is in one sense a conspectus of Spanish society during this period; for in it the painter has portrayed, with remarkable economy of means, the faces of his friends and the great men of his day, 'knights of the sad countenance' always haunted by thoughts of the next world.

Great visionary though he was, and creator of forms so strange that some went as far as to attribute them to a defect in the painter's eyesight, El Greco had a marked gift for portraiture and for rendering the essentials of a face with a few telling brushstrokes. Particularly noticeable is his ability to dispense with actual sight of the model and to make convincing portraits of the dead. Examples are the portrait of the brother of his friend Covarrubias, Bishop of Segovia, whose features, while taken over line for line from an old picture, spring amazingly to life under El Greco's brush; that of Romero de las Azanas, in which the figure is invested with something of the curious defunctive glamour of *The Burial of Count Orgaz*; and, most impressive of all, the likeness of the great Cardinal Tavera who with his livid, spectral face, deeply sunken eyes, and long white hand resting in waxen immobility on a book, looks like a figure recalled to brief life from the tomb. For achieving this strangely haunting portrayal of the dead prelate, all El Greco had to go on was the Cardinal's death mask, molded fifty years earlier by the sculptor Berruguete, who had been commissioned to build his tomb.

EL GRECO (1541-1614). THE CARDINAL OF TAVERA (AFTER 1610). (40×23½″)
HOSPITAL OF TAVERA, TOLEDO.

EL GRECO (1541-1614). SAINT ANDREW (CA. 1600). ZULOAGA MUSEUM, ZUMAYA.

In his pictures of saints (of which there are so many and which may almost be said to run in series like those of the apostles) El Greco made proof no less conspicuously of his imaginative genius, in the sense that he created for each separate saint a form corresponding to his spiritual personality. As Camon Aznar puts it, an El Greco saint seems to be rapt in expectation of his destiny. Indeed we can trace this destiny following its appointed course before our eyes. Thus in the successive portrayals of St Francis—of which there are no less than twenty-eight—we see the saintly figure growing ever more ascetic, more and more purged of all carnal attributes, until finally we see the saint's companion stricken to the ground by the awe this more-than-human presence has inspired in him.

Lost in solitary meditation or following their predestined path, these saints are sometimes grouped together by El Greco, not for hagiological reasons (as was done by the Primitives) but to stress their underlying kinship across the ages; as when, for example, he shows us St Francis in the company of St John or St Andrew. Moreover this permits him to introduce contrasting elements into his compositions, nude and fully draped figures and different builds of men. Though he imparts a symbolical aspect to each face, El Greco sometimes takes for his model a living man, and it is interesting to observe how skillfully in these cases he invests strongly realistic depictions with the attributes of sainthood. Instances of this are the various representations of St Jerome in cardinal's robes, where the saint has the haunting gaze and enormous beard of Cardinal Gaspar de Quiroga; also the pictures of St Ildefonso, that of the Escorial, in sacerdotal vestments, and the other at Illescas, in which a mild contemporary Canon is writing at the dictation of the Virgin, his face lit up with purest ecstasy as he turns towards the divine visitant. In the innumerable lawsuits with his patrons in which he was involved, El Greco was often blamed for having given saints the features

EL GRECO (1541-1614). THE VIRGIN AND APOSTLES RECEIVING THE HOLY SPIRIT.
DETAIL FROM THE PENTECOST (AFTER 1610). PRADO, MADRID.

of his friends or relatives. He is also said to have included himself in several works, notably in the group of mourners in the *Count Orgaz*. The figure which we have best grounds for thinking a self-portrait is that of the last apostle but one at the top of the picture, on the right, in *Pentecost*. Here El Greco depicts himself with complete objectivity; aloof from the general rapture, he seems to play the modest part of a lucid witness, not aspiring heavenwards but gazing straight before him, at the spectator.

The human elements which, when in isolation, are keyed up to the maximum of individual expression assume a different character when figuring in group compositions. Thus the figures of the Virgin and St John standing beside the Cross in the Prado *Crucifixion*, losing all individual characteristics, have become rhythmic elements and symbols. They are pure forms straining upwards, flamelike, etherealized, while, as in Byzantine art, the colors also have a mystical significance; untrammelled by reality, they participate in a life not of this world. In other versions the figure of the Crucified is magnified till it fills the picture; the divine tragedy has touched its climax, the tall, sinewy body flickers like a white flame among swirling clouds. The earth wholly disappears or is reduced to a faintly indicated range of hills traversed by the glimmering forms of men on horseback making their way towards Jerusalem—that is to say, Toledo. For El Greco there is the world of light, God's world, and that of darkness, ours; and this explains, no doubt, the mystery of darkness brooding over all his landscapes—except the great *View of Toledo* in 'El Greco's House.' But when showered with light from the ascending Virgin and her attendant angels, surely Toledo has acquired another significance; no longer an earthly city, symbol of this world of sadness, it has become for El Greco a holy city, the New Jerusalem.

We grasp the full meaning of these vast syntheses only when we try to see them through El Greco's eyes and bear in mind that they are not isolated works but belong to groups of interrelated paintings in which the painter's ideas attained complete visual representation. For it was in architectural settings planned by himself that at the zenith of his career (roughly between 1595 and 1605) El Greco made the large groups of pictures at the Chapel of San José and San Bernardino at Toledo, at the College of Doña Maria de Aragon and at the Hospital of the Caridad at Illescas. The pictures belonging to these groups (now wholly or partially dispersed) constitute the most lyrical portion of El Greco's output. The Madrid set of paintings which over a long period of years was the only one known to the artists and connoisseurs of the Spanish capital was also the one which suffered the most incomprehension. Visualizing that picture sequence as it originally was, we cannot fail to realize that all the scenes, when viewed as an ensemble, must have implemented a cosmic symbolism, an over-all message of profound significance. Amongst works almost certainly to be included in this group are the *Annunciation* (Museum of Villanueva y Geltru), the Prado *Baptism of Christ*, the *Adoration of the Shepherds* (formerly in the Collection of the King of Rumania) and, according to certain authorities, also the Prado *Resurrection* and *Crucifixion*, and even perhaps *Pentecost* as well. Though this last-named work may have a later date, all the others must belong to cycles of approximately the same period, and they were followed up by interesting 'variations' on the same themes, such as the *Baptism of Christ* in the Hospital of Tavera, left unfinished at the painter's death. In all this group the compositions are charged throughout with tense emotion, bodies are built up by expressive volumes that owe nothing to the world of mortal flesh, colors sing out triumphantly. Never until the coming of Cubism and Cézanne was our modern concept of pictorial architecture realized so fully and coherently—but with this difference, that in El Greco's art all the masses, even the weightiest, are swept up in a vast ascensional movement, and the linework sways and bends before a wind of inspiration. Governed by an evolution operating from within, El Greco's forms shake off the last vestiges of Baroque structure; their distortions are of another order, due to the stripping away of all but the bare essentials. In some very late works, such as *The Marriage of the Virgin* (once in the Collection of the King of Rumania) which probably came from Illescas, and the *Visitation* (Dumbarton Oaks) belonging to a closely associated cycle, or the *Vision of the Apocalypse*, all is pure abstraction; effaced by its

EL GRECO (1541-1614). VISION OF THE APOCALYPSE (CA. 1613). (88×76¼″)
ZULOAGA MUSEUM, ZUMAYA.

interpretation, the theme is merely hinted at in brief, allusive flashes striking into the heart of the mystery, yet without disclosing it, while the colors have become no more than fluent gleams, translucencies, with all that is material in them refined out of existence.

EL GRECO (1541-1614). VISION OF THE APOCALYPSE, DETAIL (CA. 1613). ZULOAGA MUSEUM, ZUMAYA.

We are often told that a distinctive trait of the Spaniard is his independence, his imperviousness to outside influences. This is hard to reconcile with the view equally current among art historians that no truly Spanish painting existed before the 17th century; that the Primitive Spanish Schools were essentially derivative. Some have claimed that El Greco could bring his personal genius to full fruition in Spain precisely because he came there at a time when indigenous art was passing through a period of sterility. In the course of our researches into Primitive Spanish art, however, we grew more and more convinced (and to such effect that this work, planned to consist of one volume, has had to be expanded into two in order to do justice to the achievement of the Spanish Primitives) that, on the contrary, there existed from the Middle Ages onward an authentically Spanish art which, while open to the new forms of art coming from abroad, proved itself capable again and again of asserting with renewed vigor its independence and originality. Thus, while the Master of Tahull impresses us by his fine sense of composition and an all-pervading rhythm, the simple poetry welling up from the heart that characterizes the work of the Master of Pedret is no less impressive. Even the humblest fresco-painters of the village churches show a gift for rendering their emotions with a poignancy and power of synthesis all but unique in early art. After studying the delicate charm of the Sienese, the Catalan painters developed an arabesque of unrivaled clearness and precision which, enveloping forms, gave them an amazing plenitude. Finally, to revert to the famous retable of Bonifacio Ferrer (which has occasioned so much controversy), I am convinced that the scenes on the side panels (illustrating *The Conversion of St Paul*, reproduced on p. 52) are by a Catalan artist, one of the group centering on the Serras (Valencian painting had obviously a Catalan origin), such is their simplicity and straightforwardness, though the predella may very well be by an Italian hand. The Valencians took over the analytic procedures of the Flemings and incorporated them in the stately, monumental constructions for which they had a natural gift; the Castilians utilized them differently but they, too, gave them an imprint of their own. Thus Jorge Inglés subordinates even the most realistic elements to a fine-spun calligraphy, so subtle that we catch ourselves thinking, surprisingly enough, of the art of the Far East.

Throughout the varied course of Spanish art we find a sort of alternation between the influence of foreign art forms welcomed with eagerness and mastered with ability and, on the other hand, manifestations of the native Spanish genius, growing ever more sure of itself as the years go by. This tidal ebb-and-flow persists from the rudimentary, archaic art of the 11th century up to the vast symphonic compositions of the Masters of the Renaissance. Thus there was a constant and fruitful interchange between complexity and simplicity, technical proficiency and instinct. So much so that it was often the Spanish artist who stood for the most abstract and international techniques, while foreign artists in Spain ended up by assimilating the traditional characteristics of Spanish art. Indeed these extra-national grafts thrived all the better for being incorporated in a vigorous parent stem.

Both tendencies were combined in El Greco and his art, after being thoroughly impregnated with that of Spain, achieved a universal quality. To such effect that the question suggests itself whether, had El Greco never lived, the evolution of Spanish art would have been the same. Seemingly all the elements of that evolution had long been in existence; far from coming on a vacant scene, El Greco made his appearance at a time when the Spanish artists were actively testing out art theories, and a revival of realistic art, on a sound, well-tried basis, was in the offing. Yet, but for El Greco, this great Spanish 17th-century school would certainly have lacked the dramatic sense of color and the bold inventiveness which delight us today. Indeed, paradoxical as this might seem, Spanish art without El Greco would strike us as more neutral, more international—in a word, less Spanish. And surely no higher praise can be accorded to a national art than that it was able thus to inspire a painter coming from another land; and to El Greco than that, despite his originality and strength of character, he made proof of a mind so comprehensive, so pregnantly discerning.

BIOGRAPHICAL
AND
BIBLIOGRAPHICAL NOTICES
BY
A. BUSUIOCEANU

INDEX OF NAMES

BIOGRAPHIES

BASSA, FERRER (?-1348).

In March, 1315, King Alfonso IV of Aragon issued a pardon to one Ferrer Baço, citizen of Tortosa, for the rape of three maidens in that city; the queen herself interceded in the accused's favor. Again, five years later, one Ferrer Bassa of Sasgaioles (a town near Barcelona), charged with a serious crime and sentenced to exile and confiscation of all his property, was pardoned by the same king. We have no proof that the delinquent in each case was the painter Bassa. But when the truth is undiscoverable, history falls back on such coincidences and one is tempted to call on the painter to prove himself "not guilty". Little is known of his life. Born probably between 1285 and 1290, he seems to have learned a good deal from Italian art and is to Catalan painting what Giotto and Simone Martini, his contemporaries, are to Italian. He was employed by Pedro IV El Ceremonioso, King of Aragon, and in records from 1324 on there is frequent mention of Bassa, steadily at work on altarpieces in Catalonia, Aragon and Roussillon. All these are lost today, except for one, the sole work by which we can judge the artist: this is a group of murals, painted in oils in 1345-1346, decorating the cloister of the Convent of Pedralbes, near Barcelona. Ferrer Bassa died in 1348 while at work on an altarpiece illustrating the life of St Francis, for the Franciscan Convent at Valencia.

BERMEJO, BARTOLOMÉ (?-after 1498).

During Jaime Huguet's last years his only rival at Barcelona was a Cordovan painter, Bartolomé de Cardenas, better known as Bartolomé Bermejo, and sometimes (after one of his signatures, the Latin version of his name) as Bartholomeus Rubeus. No records are extant prior to the time when he was working in Aragon and Barcelona. Some have believed that he visited Seville and even traveled to Flanders and Italy, where he developed his artistic personality and brilliant technique: but this is only conjecture. It is thought (no proof exists) that he worked at Valencia as a youth. What is certain is that in 1474 he was a painter of considerable renown in Aragon. One of his major works, the *St Dominic of Silos* in the Prado, was part of an altarpiece which he made about that time for the altar of this Saint at Daroca. In the same town he painted a *Pietà*, assisted by the Aragonese painter Martin Bernat, as well as other paintings that have not come down to us. In 1477 he was busy working at Saragossa, imitated by the Aragonese painters and sometimes aided by his pupils. It was he who introduced oil painting to Aragon. We find him at Barcelona for the first time in 1486, competing with Jaime Huguet for a commission which, in the end, fell to neither of them. In 1490 he finished the admirable *Pietà*, painted for Canon Despla, now in the Cathedral of Barcelona. He designed some stained-glass windows for the Cathedral in 1495 and in 1498 he was employed at Vich. His two finest works are the *St Dominic* of the Prado and the Despla *Pietà*. These give us a good idea of his personality as an artist and enable us to ascribe to him other paintings, in Barcelona, in England *(St Michael)* and the United States *(Santa Engracia)*. Two of his leading works are in Italy: a *Virgin with Donor*, signed, in the Cathedral of Acqui and a *Saint Catherine* in the Pisa Museum.

BERRUGUETE, PEDRO (?-1504).

Much influenced in the 15th century by Flemish art, Castilian painting reached its peak point in the last quarter of the century with Pedro Berruguete, a disciple of the Italians. He was born at Paredes de Nava, near Palencia in Old Castile. The only exact dates we have regarding him relate to the very last years of his life. He is believed to have started his career as a pupil of Fernando Gallego, who was then working at Palencia; but it is certain that he perfected his talent by contact with the best Italian painters of the day. Indeed there is every reason to believe that the 'Pedro the Spaniard' who worked with Melozzo da Forli at Urbino in 1477 for Duke Federigo da Montefeltro was none other then Berruguete. Ascribed to him (in collaboration with Justus of Ghent) is a series of prophets and philosophers painted for the Castle of Urbino and now at the Galleria Barberini in Rome, at the Louvre and at Windsor Castle. He seems to have left Italy soon after the death of Duke Federigo in 1482; we hear of him in Spain for the first time after that date. Between 1483 and 1495 he was painting some murals, now lost, for Toledo Cathedral. Soon after, he migrated to Avila where, from 1499 until his death, he was employed on works for the Convent of St Thomas and the Cathedral. It is these works of his last years that reveal his talent at its splendid best, his masterpiece being the altar picture in the Convent of St Thomas illustrating the life of the Saint. Other paintings, panels from altarpieces in the same convent devoted to the lives of *St Thomas* and *St Peter Martyr*, are now in the Prado. The artist was at work on an altarpiece for the Cathedral of Avila when he died towards the end of 1503 or the beginning of 1504. He left this picture unfinished; it was continued by Santa Cruz and completed by Juan de Borgoña. Pedro was the father of Alonso Berruguete, a sculptor, architect and painter who is esteemed the Michelangelo of Spain.

BORRASSA, LUIS (?-ca. 1424).

In the crowded annals of Catalan Primitive painting at the end of the 14th century and the beginning of the 15th, the name Borrassá crops up again and again. It may be that all these artists belonged to the same family. Outstanding, and leader of a school, was Luis, a native of Gerona and probably the son of Guillermo Borrassá, a painter who worked in the cathedral of that town between 1360 and 1399. The first reference to Luis dates from 1380. He had yet to establish himself and was then at work restoring stained-glass windows in the cathedral of his native town. Eight years later, however, we find him a successful artist running his own studio at Barcelona. Juan I, King of Aragon, summoned him to Saragossa to lend a hand in the coronation festivities. He then entered on a period of great activity and enjoyed ever-increasing renown. He was employed by the King and his works were eagerly sought for by cathedrals and convents throughout Catalonia. The modern of his day, he sponsored the new style of art, now known as International Gothic. His sudden fame eclipsed that of the Serra brothers, in whose studio an outmoded tradition was still respected. Works incontestably his are the altarpiece of Guardiola (1404), now in the Museum of Barcelona, that in the Church of Santa Maria at Tarrasa (1411) and those of Vich (1415) and Seva (1418), both of which are in the Museum of Vich. Borrassá had a number of pupils, several of whom bore his name.

COELLO, ALONSO SANCHEZ (1531/32-1590).

At the time when the work of that humble, provincial artist, Luis Morales, was in high favor with the populace, another painter, Sanchez Coello, the portraitist, was basking in the favor of King

Philip's court and winning commendation from the poet Lope de Vega, as "Spain's glorious first-born artist." Strictly speaking, this perfect courtier, luxury-lover and cosmopolitan, was not a Spaniard, for he was of Portuguese extraction, though born in Spain at Benifayo, near Valencia, round about 1531. He was educated in Flanders and Portugal in a *milieu* which facilitated his rapid rise to fame. Antonio Moro, the Dutch portrait-painter, whom he had first met in Brussels or in Lisbon, took him under his wing, trained him, and helped him on his path. It was probably thanks to Moro, King's Painter to Charles V, that when quite a young man he was invited for the first time to Valladolid (in 1552). There he made a portrait of the Infanta Juana, whose hand was promised to Don Juan of Portugal, Prince of Brazil, and was commissioned to paint further portraits of the royal family in Lisbon. He returned to Valladolid in 1557 and stayed there. This was the time when Moro, as a result of indiscretions, was falling out of favor with the king; indeed, before long, he had to beat a hasty retreat from the Spanish court. Coello stepped into his place. True, he was grieved at losing a friend (as a biographer puts it, himself perhaps a courtier), but this loss was the artist's gain, for (continues the biographer) he was thus enabled to devote his talent wholly to the service of a very great king. He soon became the favorite of Philip II, who addressed him in his letters as "my very dear son." He was the bosom friend of princes and infantes, honored in foreign courts and cherished by two successive popes. What is more, he proved himself worthy of the confidence placed in him and never spared himself in his efforts to gratify the king's tastes and meet his wishes. Mediocre as a religious painter, he was the faithful interpreter of a court that delighted in polished, accurate pictures of itself. He left an extensive gallery of portraits, the best of which are now in the Prado, in the Covent of the 'Descalzas Reales' and in numerous collections and foreign art museums, notably in Vienna and Dublin. Coello set the tone of the painting of his day. He died in Madrid, in 1590.

DALMAU, Luis (?-ca. 1460).

This painter, who studied directly under Jan van Eyck, had every chance of becoming for Catalan painting what, at almost the same time, Nuño Gonsalves became for Portuguese painting. But something was lacking in his temperament: the sacred fire or, perhaps, the driving force required for his high destiny. He seems to have been a native of Valencia. He was living in 1420 and was still there in 1428, when we find him in the service of Alfonso V, King of Aragon. Next year he received an expense allowance from the royal treasury for journeys in Castile in connection with the marriage of the King's brother. It was at this time that Jan van Eyck visited Spain and Portugal as the Duke of Burgundy's envoy. An embassy from Philip the Good had preceded the Flemish painter in 1427, passing through Valencia on their way back to Burgundy. Dalmáu may have turned these circumstances to useful account, for in 1431 he was sent to Flanders by the king, doubtless in order to perfect his knowledge of painting. How long he stayed or how he spent his time is not known. However, the sole work ascribed to him with certainty—the central panel of the altarpiece of the *Virgin of the Councillors* in the Museum of Barcelona—supports the view that he worked in the Van Eycks' studio and carefully studied their methods. He seems to have found particular inspiration in the angels of the Saint Bavon altarpiece, finished in 1432. Back in Spain in 1436, he stayed again at Valencia until 1438 or later. Five years after, we find him at Barcelona, where he was commissioned to make the *Virgin of the Councillors* altarpiece. He signed this work in 1445. In 1460

he was in the service of the new king, Juan II. This is the last we hear of him; that year the plague was raging at Barcelona.

FERNANDEZ, Alejo (?-1543).

Brother of the sculptor Jorge Fernandez (or Hernandez), also known as *Aleman*, this painter was perhaps of German descent. The place and date of his birth are unknown. Perhaps he came from Seville—but he was certainly living at Cordova in 1498 when he married for the first time. There is no record of his early years, his teachers, the journeys he may have made. Much research has been devoted to elucidating both his obvious kinship with painters from Bruges and Venice and, at the same time, that archaic element in his work which makes him seem a belated 16th-century Primitive. He worked at Cordova until 1508, but none of the work he did there has survived. That year he and his brother were called to Seville to work on a big altarpiece for the High Altar of the cathedral. His chief works date from this time: the *Maese Rodrigo* altarpiece in the University Chapel, the fine group of paintings from the *Nicolas Durango* altarpiece (1509-1513) in the Cathedral, and the famous *Virgin of the Navigators* in the Alcazar at Seville. It would be attractive to identify among the group kneeling in the shelter of the Virgin's mantle one or other of the great sea-venturers, Christopher Columbus or his son; unhappily these are only likenesses of the ship-builders and merchants of Seville who financed the voyages of discovery and commissioned the picture. Fernandez was not only a highly successful painter, not only a miniaturist and gilder of statuary, but he also had a fine gift for decoration. On the occasion of the entry of Charles V into Seville in 1526, he was put in charge of the decorations of the city and set up huge triumphal arches in the Italian manner, crowned with statues and allegorical figures. There remains no record of his activities after 1528. He died at an advanced age at Seville, in 1543. His son Sebastian, also a painter, imitated his father's style.

GALLEGO, Fernando (?-after 1507).

We know little about this painter, who worked in Castile during the second half of the 15th century and had pupils and imitators in many parts of Spain. In 1468 he is known to have been painting in the Cathedral of Palencia with one Juan Felipe. In 1473 he was at Coria where he undertook to do six retables for the Cathedral. Assisted by Pedro de Tolosa, he painted the Gallery of the University Chapel at Salamanca in 1507. None of these paintings has survived and there remain but a few signed works displaying Gallego's authentic style and enabling us to distinguish between the master and his school. The oldest in date, and a key-work in the early phase of the Castilian School, is the altarpiece of *St Ildefonso*, painted shortly before 1467 for Cardinal Juan de Mella, in the Cathedral of Zamora. Here Gallego showed himself a disciple of the Flemish painters, owing much to Dirck Bouts, or perhaps to works of that master's school. He painted with vigor, his originality consisting in a strongly marked realism, a predilection for harsh, rustic types of humanity, a rigid, angular treatment of forms and, in particular, of drapery. The altarpiece in the Chapel of St Anthony at the New Cathedral of Salamanca was painted somewhat later. The influence of Martin Schongauer's prints is perceptible in this work—as indeed in most Castilian painting of the period. Two other outstanding pictures in the Weibel Collection in Madrid probably came from this altarpiece. Only one is signed: a large *Pietà*, whose emotionalism recalls Rogier van der Weyden, although Gallego treats the subject in a harsher manner. Despite the stark, monumental rigidity of his forms there is very real feeling in his work. His *Calvary*, on the other hand, from the same collection, almost overdoes the dramatic possibilities of the scene, the agonized expressions of the faces. Another artist, Francisco Gallego, whose style is much like that of Fernando, painted (in 1500) the altarpiece of *St Catherine* at the Old Cathedral of Salamanca. The work has so much in common with Fernando Gallego's mature style that we must assume this painter to have worked in close association with the master; perhaps he was his brother or his son.

EL GRECO, DOMINICO THEOTOKOPULI, called (1541-1614).

El Greco's life is shrouded in mystery. He was a riddle to his contemporaries and remains so to those who study his work today. He was a Greek, born in Crete (perhaps in 1541), but we know nothing of his family or even his exact place of birth. Very young, he learnt the painter's craft from monks and worked on icons. Hope of greater things drew him to Italy, first to Venice (when exactly is not known) where he studied the great masters of the day. Later, at Rome and in Spain, he passed for a pupil of Titian, but his painting is closer to that of Tintoretto and Bassano. From Venice he went to Parma, then in 1570 to Rome. There Giulio Clovio (almost his fellow-countryman) gave him an introduction to Cardinal Farnese. He soon made a great name for himself and even had some pupils. But his views on art were far from orthodox and, as a result of some slighting remarks he made about Michelangelo when in the Sistine Chapel, he found himself obliged to leave Rome. Attracted perhaps by the prospect of working for Philip II at the Escorial, he now set out for Spain. Did he stop at Malta or sail directly to a Spanish port? Nothing is known of the date or circumstances of his arrival in Spain, the land whither his destiny was calling him. It is at Toledo that we first have news of him: when in 1577 he signed a contract for the large altarpiece of the Church of Santo Domingo El Antiguo. He had yet to learn Spanish; he still expressed himself in Italian and he signed his pictures in Greek characters—this latter a habit he kept to the end of his life. He was not alone for long, for while at Toledo in 1578 he had a son, Jorge Manuel, by Doña Jeronima de las Cuevas. He seems to have been deeply attached to this lady, whose face with its delicately sensual charm he has immortalized in many of his pictures of the 'Virgin and Child.' They were never officially married, however—a breach of the conventions which Spanish historians refuse to believe possible at Toledo in the sixteenth century. El Greco's life was unconventional throughout. The mere fact of his coming to Toledo was remarkable enough, and equally so his staying on there, for though he was admired, he was rarely understood. When he made his famous *Espolio* (1579) for the Cathedral, he was blamed for the liberties he took in painting Christ, giving Him a tunic of too bright a red to figure in a sacred edifice and surrounding Him with 'Holy Women' (amongst them Doña Jeronima) much too 'profane' in their appearance. In fact the Chapter was frankly scandalized. Thus the stakes were high when, in 1580 at the Escorial, he painted another masterpiece, *The Martyrdom of St Maurice*. And it was now the King who disapproved. Just as the painter had overdone the red in the picture at Toledo Cathedral, so here he had overdone his blues and yellows, and, to make things worse, had relegated the essential action, the martyrdom of the Forty Thousand, to the background. He returned to Toledo, never to leave it again. He had lost his chance of becoming an official painter, but he had won his freedom. At Santo Tomé in 1586 El Greco painted his *Burial of Count Orgaz*, first of a series of masterpieces in which he gave free rein to his 'eccentricities.' Though his works were bought for their undeniable charm, the world looked upon him as a madman. But El Greco cared nothing for the opinion of others. There was also talk of his defective eyesight, to explain the 'inaccuracy' of his drawing. When in the course of a lawsuit he was taken to task for unduly elongating figures, he retorted disconcertingly: "To be dwarfed is the worst thing that can happen to any form." Shortly before his death, a fellow-artist, Pacheco, came from Seville to visit him—and a visit to El Greco was well worth the journey. He asked El Greco's opinion of Michelangelo. "A worthy man," was the reply, "but he never knew how to paint." This view, which he had been airing since his youth, never failed to shock his hearers—it was little short of blasphemy! All the same he was appreciated and understood by an élite. Lope de Vega had no word of praise for him; but Gongora wrote a sonnet upon his death in 1614, and the Jesuit Paravicino, of whom he made a magnificent portrait, wrote others. Velazquez, too, was a firm believer in his genius.

HUGUET, JAIME (?-1492).

After the middle of the 15th century, the lead in Catalan painting passed from Martorell's studio to that of Jaime Huguet. Jaime was probably the son of Pedro Huguet, a native of Valls in the province of Tarragona and a painter in a small way, who is known to have been working in Barcelona Cathedral between 1434 and 1448. It is believed that Jaime lived in Aragon between 1440 and 1447, and it was there that he painted his most attractive works. After a brief stay at Tarragona, he was in Barcelona in 1448 and from then until 1486 we find frequent references to his activities, which were considerable, for he was nothing if not prolific. He made his studio not only the center to which painters throughout Catalonia and a part of Aragon looked for guidance, but also a kind of picture-factory—and in the end this affected his art injuriously. He employed a great number of apprentices and had to call in other painters to cope with the orders showered on him, none of which he ever refused. Among his collaborators were his brother Antonio Huguet, Miguel Nadal and Pedro Ramirez of Saragossa. He kept in close touch with the Vergos, a family of painters who did much for the decorative *facture* of his pictures. Now ascribed to him are several works in Saragossa Museum, the famous panel of *St George and the Princess* in Barcelona Museum and the small altarpiece of the *Epiphany* in the Museum of Vich, in addition to the large-scale, later works: the *St Anthony Abbot* altarpiece (destroyed by fire in 1909); the altarpiece of *Saints Abdon and Sennen* at Tarrasa (1460); that of Constable Don Pedro de Portugal (1465) in the museum of the Royal Chapel of St Agueda at Barcelona; the altarpiece of *St Vincent* of Sarria in Barcelona Museum, painted at two different times; that of *St Bernardin and the Guardian Angel* at Barcelona Cathedral (1468-1469); and that of *Saint Augustine* in Barcelona Museum, of which only the central panel, the *Consecration of the Saint*, is positively ascribed to him. Many records of his public and private activities are extant. Huguet died in 1492.

JACOMART, JAIME BAÇO, alias (ca. 1413-1461).

A contemporary of Luis Dalmáu and the Catalan Martorell, Jacomart was the most highly esteemed painter in Valencia in the middle period of the 15th century and enjoyed the favor of the King. His real name was Jaime Baço, but the records always add *alias Jacomart* or *Mestre Jacomart*, which suggests that the family hailed from Picardy. He was the son of a court tailor. We know nothing of his early years, but he had certainly made his name when in 1440 King Alfonso V of Aragon summoned him by letter to Naples, while laying siege to that city for the second time. But Jacomart, busily at work in Valencia, was disinclined to move. In 1442, while directing the third siege of Naples, the king nominated Jacomart "chief painter of the Court" and sent him an urgent summons. Thus at last Jacomart came to Naples. In September 1444 he finished a painting on wood of such proportions that ten men were needed to move it. This work perished in another war. Back in Valencia, he was again (in 1446) called to Italy, where the king was investing other cities. Next year, at Tivoli, Jacomart painted twenty banners for the army and a gonfalon for the king. In 1451 he was back in Valencia, loaded with work and with honors. In 1456, though now wholly Italian in his tastes, the king confirmed Jacomart's post of Court Painter and authorized him to make use of the royal coat-of-arms in his own house. Jacomart went on working in the Cathedral of Valencia, in the Royal Chapel and elsewhere, but none of these works has survived. Reliable documentary information is available regarding one painting only: the altarpiece in the church at Cati, for which he signed a contract in 1461. With this work as a pointer, others have been ascribed to the artist. Unfortunately Jacomart died that very year, 1461, and this painting is now known to be by the hand of Juan Reixach, his friend and pupil. But such surprises are the all-too-frequent lot of the art-historian—artists known only by what can be gleaned from the works of others, shadows of their own.

JUANES, JUAN DE (ca. 1523-1579).

He is believed to have been born at Fuente la Higuera, near Valencia, in 1523 or a little earlier. He started life with the name of his father, Juan Vicente Masip, but later styled himself Juan de Juanes, perhaps because of some vague connection with the noble family of that name, whose coat-of-arms he used. His last Will and Testament is the only documentary record we have of him. He was working in the church of Bocairente, near Valencia, in 1579 when he fell ill and made this will. He died at the end of the year. He was a pupil of his father, with whom he collaborated until 1550. He seems to have traveled little. The Italianate style of the father was carried on by the son and his cult of Raphael led him to a mannerist type of art in which exaggeratedly dramatic movement was combined with mawkish tenderness of expression. We may be sure he admired the Flemish painters for their piety, for devoutness was the keynote of all his painting. He enjoyed vast popularity and some of his pictures—like the *Last Supper* and the *Savior* in the Prado—became veritable objects of worship. At Valencia one of his *Virgins* was credited with working miracles. Thus a halo of piety surrounds the figure of Juan de Juanes. Tradition has it that he partook of the Sacrament before beginning any work intended for a church. His best pictures are those at Valencia, among them the *Mystical Marriage of the Venerable Agnesio* in the Museum, and the *Last Supper* in the Church of San Nicolas. The painter had three children, Vicente-Juan, Dorotea and Margarita, all of them painters and disciples of their father.

MARTORELL, BERNARDO (?-1453/55).

A painter and miniaturist whose work has only recently come into prominence, Martorell is looked upon today as the leading Catalan painter of the second quarter of the 15th century. He is often mentioned in contemporary records and we gather that after 1433 he was highly reputed as an artist and had a very busy studio. His works, however, long remained unknown or doubtfully ascribed, and his personality was overshadowed by that of a mysterious rival, the 'Master of St George,' painter of the altarpiece of *St George* now divided

up between the Louvre and the Chicago Museum. However some recently discovered records prove that it was Martorell who painted (in 1437) the altarpiece of San Pedro in the small town of Pubol, near Ampurias, and in the light of this discovery we can not only form a clearer idea of the artist's personality but also can assign to him a whole series of notable paintings—among them the *St George* altarpiece mentioned above. Hence a triumphant come-back for Martorell and a feather in the cap of the art-historians. Also ascribed to him are several large altarpieces in the Museum of Vich and that of the *Transfiguration* in Barcelona Cathedral (1447). A document dating from 1448 mentions Martorell as a miniaturist; however, the illuminated page he undertook to make for the codex of Jaime Marquilles' *Commentaris* does not seem to be by his hand. Towards the end of his life Martorell was snowed under with orders. He had many pupils and was busily at work when he died at Barcelona between 1453 and 1455. In 1456 another painter, Pedro Garcia de Benabarre, probably his pupil, took over his studio for five years and undertook to complete the master's unfinished works.

MASIP, JUAN VICENTE (?-ca. 1550).

There was a Masip atelier at Valencia in the 16th century and a whole dynasty of painters by this name. The founder of this 'school,' which occupied the same studio for nearly three-quarters of a century, was Juan Vicente Masip, a notable artist and devotee of Raphael and the great Italians. His very existence was unknown until comparatively recently, his figure having been overshadowed by his famous son who bore the same name, though more usually known as Juan de Juanes. Masip was probably born in the last quarter of the 15th century. In 1513 he was working in Valencia and must have known Yañez and Llanos, whose influence is plain to see in all his work, though the dominant quality of his painting is its 'Raphaelism.' Pictures unquestionably his are those in the Cathedral of Segorbe, which he finished between 1531 and 1535. From now on he seems to have usually worked with his son. A *Baptism* (1535) in the Cathedral of Valencia and several pictures in the Prado are ascribed to him. There is no hope of distinguishing his share—doubtless a considerable one—in the pictures jointly painted by himself and his son. Masip died at Valencia about 1550.

MORALES, LUIS (?-1586).

Morales was a native of Badajoz, a city in the poverty-stricken province of Estremadura, a breeding-ground for conquistadors but not, until Morales, for artists. He was probably born in the first quarter of the 16th century, for his first son was baptised at Badajoz in 1554. Nothing is known of his social background or how he spent his youth. Some early biographers mention the Flemish painter Pedro de Campaña (Pieter de Kempeneer) and artists of Valladolid and Toledo as his teachers, but no proof of this exists. Living so near Portugal he may have known the Portuguese Primitives as well as the Flemish paintings so much prized in that country. He was one of the few Spanish artists invited by Philip II to work at the Escorial. Asked to submit a trial picture for the king's approval, he painted a *Christ bearing the Cross*, a theme typical of his liking for pious, popular subjects. But the work was not to the king's taste and Morales was dismissed with a compensation for his pains. His *Christ* went not to the Escorial but to the Church of St Jerome in Madrid, where it remains today. To this setback, in its way not unlike El Greco's with the same judges, may perhaps be attributed the humility and sadness of the painter's outlook on life. He resumed his production of sorrowful Virgins, Pietàs, Ecce Homos for the churches of his native province and its pious homes. He never left Badajoz again, worked hard and always remained poor. A legend tells of a last meeting with King Philip when the King passed through Badajoz in 1581, after his subjugation of Portugal. Seeing the painter, the King remarked: "Indeed you are very old, Morales." "Yes, Sire," he replied, "and very poor." Whereupon the King granted him a pension of 300 ducats. But Morales did not enjoy it long, for he died in 1586. The writers of the period did not think highly of him, but the public greatly liked his pictures. They preserved them with reverent care and even named the painter "El Divino Morales."

MUR RAMON DE (?-after 1435).

The imposing Altarpiece of Guimera (painted between 1402 and 1412 and now in the Museum of Vich) had long been recognized as the work of some outstanding painter, and a whole group of paintings in more or less the same style gave rise to such designations as the 'Guimera manner' and the 'Master of Guimera'. This artist, while seeming to belong to Catalan art of the period of Luis Borrassá, obviously stemmed from a tradition other than Borrassá's. Recent investigation, however, has identified the painter of the Altarpiece of Guimera as Ramón de Mur, a hitherto unknown Catalan artist. His name came to light in documents relating to another work: the altarpiece of *St Peter* at Vinaixa, done in 1420, now in the Museum of Tarragona. He was living at Tarrega in 1421. In 1432 he was commissioned to do another painting for Vinaixa. In 1435 he made a second contract for this work—an altarpiece dedicated to the *St Johns* —but for some reason we do not know the work was finally done by Bernardo Martorell. Also ascribed to Ramón de Mur is the altar picture of Cervera, now in the Museum of Barcelona; this probably dates from some time after the Altarpiece of Guimera. This artist, unlike Borrassá, remained closely attached to the traditions of 14th-century painting. He had a commanding personality and his pictures reveal an art at once sedate and vigorous, in which Catalan critics see an eloquent expression of deep-seated national characteristics. Ramón's style is not without reminiscences of contemporary Aragonese painting. Hence the conjecture that he may have received his training in the studio of Lorenzo de Zaragoza.

NAVARRETE, JUAN FERNANDEZ DE (EL MUDO) (1526-1579).

A contemporary of Sanchez Coello, Luis Morales and El Greco, Navarrete was the only Spanish painter invited by Philip II to work at the Escorial —a signal proof of the esteem in which the King held him. The artist was born at Logroño in 1526. A deaf-mute from childhood, he studied painting in his native province, and though his training was of the most haphazard kind his talent soon gained him a certain reputation. None of his early work is extant. His first biographer, Fray José de Siguenza, states—and this has been generally echoed—that Navarrete studied in Italy and was a pupil of Titian. No record of his presence in Italy has been found, however, and the first work he submitted for the King's approval—*The Baptism* (1568), now in the Prado—has not the least resemblance to Titian or the Venetian School, but is an academic work with little character of its own, done in the Italianate manner of the period and displaying, rather, Florentine and Roman influences. In any case the picture pleased the King, who at once appointed the artist Court Painter. From now on Navarrete showed a marked fondness for Titian, whose works he copied at the Escorial. He also studied Correggio and Bassano. Indeed, it must be said that the echoes of other painters in his art are remarkably varied and show a mind open to such

widely different styles of painting as those of Hieronymus Bosch, Joachim Patinir and El Greco, Navarrete's young contemporary. What he lacked in originality, Navarrete to some extent made up for by the openmindedness and gift of assimilation that make him an eclectic painter, typical of the taste then in vogue at the Escorial. (His entire known *œuvre* is, in fact, comprised by the pictures he made for that august building.) The color in his *St Jerome* (1569) is reminiscent of Venice, though the meticulous treatment of the landscape and the painter's insistence on anecdotal elements, with the animals figuring in the scene, rather bring to mind the Flemish painters. More subtle effects of light are to be found in *The Martyrdom of St James* (1571). Other pictures finished before 1575—notably *The Birth of Jesus* and *The Carrying of the Body of Saint Lawrence*, works inspired by Correggio and Bassano—are studies in the rendering of nocturnal and artificial light. In *The Flagellation* he harked back to the Romanism then in fashion. Sometimes, as in *The Holy Family*, he indulged his predilection for animal painting and this, though it pleased the public, was severely criticized by his more orthodox contemporaries. His last works, painted in 1577 and 1578, were eight pictures representing the Evangelists and the Apostles. Thirty-two had been commissioned in all for the altars of the Basilica; and as the artist was known for his tendency to "whimsy," as Fray Siguenza put it, he was expressly forbidden to include any cats or dogs in the pictures —a prohibition which Navarrete duly respected. He produced a series of noble figures obviously inspired by his admiration for the Florentines and Venetians. He was very ill at this time, however, and retired to Toledo in 1579, where he died the same year. The work on the pictures he left unfinished was completed by Sanchez Coello and Luis de Carvajal.

OSONA, RODRIGO DE (?-after 1510).

Rodrigo was the leading painter in Valencia during the last quarter of the 15th century, though it is not known whether he was actually Valencian by birth. He is first mentioned in 1476 when the Vicar-General Juan Albarraci commissioned him to make a retable for the Church of San Nicolas at Valencia. In 1483-1484 he was working for Cardinal Borgia and his name appears in records up to 1510. Though Rodrigo was a busy, successful artist, almost the whole of his output has been lost. Only after the identification of the retable at San Nicolas, a signed work, as incontestably his, have we gained some idea of his personality. In it the artist appears to bridge two periods, still harking back to the Flemish painters, but blending with that tradition the new strains of the Italian Renaissance—and thus foreshadowing the art of the Italianate Flemings to come. Attention is often drawn to his affinities with Hugo van der Goes and the likelihood of his contact with the 15th-century artists of Northern Italy, in particular the Paduans. But there is more in his art than a merely composite style; for the essence of Rodrigo's painting is its typically Spanish realism and a characteristic hint of sadness in his emotional expression and color, which suggest an Andalusian background. Thus we feel he had a richer personality than Jacomart's, whose art, while pleasing to the eye and decorative, goes no farther. Unfortunately, no reconstitution of Rodrigo's *œuvre* is possible as yet, though a group of paintings in the Johnson Collection at Philadelphia has been ascribed to him; also (though more doubtfully) a picture at the Prado entitled *The Virgin with the Knight of Montesa*, an *Adoration of the Magi* at Bayonne and an *Annunciation* in a German collection. The artist had a son, also called Rodrigo, who worked in the same style, but lacked his father's skill. His best work is an *Epiphany* in the National Gallery,

London, signed *lo fill de Maestre Rodrigo*. Other paintings by him as well as several works of his father's school are in the Museum of Valencia. Rodrigo de Osona's studio was in active production at Valencia for nearly half a century.

PACHECO, Francisco (1564-1654).

Painter and man of letters, Pacheco was Velazquez' teacher and also his father-in-law. And it was he who interviewed El Greco at Toledo. These, we may say, are his chief titles to fame. Born in 1564 at Sanlucar de Barrameda, he was reared at Seville by his uncle, Canon Francisco Pacheco, a maker of Latin verses and scholar of note who passed on his literary tastes to his nephew. He learned the rudiments of painting from a second-rank artist, Luis Fernandez, who set him to copying works by the Fleming Pedro de Campaña and the Sevillian Luis de Vargas. An addict of Roman mannerism, he conceived a passion for Raphael, though his first-hand knowledge of Italian art was limited to copies and prints. Only twice in his lifetime did he leave Seville. In 1611 he traveled to Madrid and Toledo, where he was shocked at finding El Greco's art at variance with Aristotle's laws and styled his pictures *crueles borrones* (brutal sketches). He made another trip to Madrid in 1623 with Velazquez, his son-in-law, who as Court Painter was in a position to make his stay agreeable and worthwhile. He lingered in the capital for two years, then returned to Seville where he devoted himself to his painting and literary works. He also kept a vigilant eye on others' painting, for, as a learned iconographer and a doctrinarian, he was appointed official censor of the Inquisition. His own pictures may be seen in Seville. They break no rules; are dry, cold, soporific. He did, however, leave behind a work of great iconographic value, though unfinished: his Compendium of True Portraits of Illustrious and Memorable Men, containing 170 portraits in black and red crayon, accompanied by biographies. He also left a treatise on theory and technique, his *Arte de la Pintura*, published in 1649 and containing biographies of artists. Pacheco died at Seville in 1654. Contemporary writers lavished eulogies on him, though their opinion seems not to have been shared by all the Sevillians who saw his pictures. One of them, indeed, went so far as to affix to the feet of a naked Christ by Pacheco an epigram in verse, running as follows:

Who has made Thee so,
My Lord, so wan and lifeless?
Thou wilt say "Tis Love."
"Nay," say I ; "Pacheco!"

PANTOJA DE LA CRUZ, Juan (1551-1608).

Born at Madrid in 1551, he was Coello's disciple and, like him, a court painter. His biographers have much to say of his precocious talent. His docility is also noteworthy, for he followed exactly in the footsteps of his master and carefully conformed to the tastes of the King. Like Coello, he made many copies for the King—mostly of portraits by Titian and Moro—and he spared no pains in learning to combine accuracy with punctilious decorum. Though he lacked Coello's skill, he was much appreciated by Philip II. An indifferent painter of religious subjects, he excelled in his portraits, the best of which are in the Prado, the Escorial and the Castle of Raudnitz in Bohemia. In the portrait of Philip II at the Escorial, his masterpiece, he portrays the old king with accuracy and—what is rarer in his work—with psychological insight, making us feel the melancholy of the king's declining years. Other excellent portraits are those of Philip III, Don Francisco Gutierrez de Cuellar (in the Cathedral of Segovia) and Fray Hernando Rojas (in a private collection). The painter died in Madrid in 1608.

He too won a posthumous eulogy from the pen of Lope de Vega, who likened him to an Apelles whose "beautiful colors would have awed Apollo himself." Whereas his palette strikes us today very differently—as cold and somber.

REIXACH, Juan (?-after 1484).

It is impossible to say for certain whether this name applied to one artist only or to two artists flourishing at about the same time. The earliest mention we have of a painter of this name tells of his being at Saragossa in 1431. He worked for various churches at Valencia and, between 1436 and 1439, for the Royal Palace of Jativa. In the chapel of the Palace the Valencian Luis Dalmáu made a painting (in 1436) for an altarpiece by Juan Reixach. The name crops up again in 1443 when a Juan Reixach made the valuation of an altarpiece painted by Jacomart for the Church of Bujarsot. This second Reixach, whether or not the same man as the first, is referred to in documents between 1443 and 1484. He was a disciple and collaborator of Jacomart. Work by his hand has been distinguished in the altar picture of St Martin, at Segorbe, ascribed to Jacomart and dated 1447 or 1457 (now in Segorbe Museum). He it was, too, who made the altarpiece in the Church of Cati, for which Jacomart signed a contract in 1461, shortly before his death. We get a better idea of Reixach from the only signed and dated work that has come down to us: the altarpiece of *St Ursula*, painted for the Church of Cubells in 1468 (and now in Barcelona Museum). Here Reixach docilely follows in his master's steps. He took over his manner, his types of figures and his methods of composition to a point that makes it difficult to sort out the work of each. Also ascribed to Reixach is the altarpiece of the *Magi* in the Augustinian Convent at Rubielos de Mora, a work of considerable merit and remarkably fine color. The artist is last mentioned in 1484, alongside the Valencian painter Pedro Cabanes. When he died is not known.

RIBALTA, Francisco (1551/55-1628).

Little is known of Ribalta's life. A contemporary of Caravaggio, he pointed the way to the Golden Age of Spanish painting in the 17th century. Born in 1551 or 1555 (the records are conflicting) at Castellon de la Plana, in the province of Valencia, he was of Catalan extraction, but lived at Valencia, and fell in line with the art traditions of that center. In his youth, he was vastly impressed by the work of Juan de Juanes and the man himself. Early biographers say that he studied in Italy and was a disciple of the Carracci. Of this no proof exists and Ribalta's painting shows no signs of their eclecticism. However this may be, he was in Madrid in 1582; a picture in the Hermitage at Leningrad, signed and dated, proves it. Though he had no official post, he probably frequented the court painters; also he seems to have copied pictures by Raphael and Sebastiano del Piombo at the Escorial, and thus to have come in contact with Italian art. Navarrete el Mudo, whose influence is obvious in some of his paintings, was a great friend of his. It was doubtless at this time, and in court circles, that he encountered Lope de Vega, who wrote verses in Ribalta's praise and whose portrait he painted in 1614. Exactly when he returned to Valencia is uncertain; but he was back in 1597 and spent the rest of his life there. At Valencia, between 1601 and 1607, he made the important group of pictures in the College of the Patriachate and, in 1603, those in the Church of Algemesi. He was behind the launching of the 'College of Painters' at Valencia, to promoting which he devoted much energy between 1607 and 1617. His last works and those most typical of his fully evolved style are the paintings done between 1625 and 1627 at the

Monastery of Portacoeli; they are now in Valencia Museum. Ribalta died in 1628. He had a son, Juan Ribalta, painter and poet, who died young. He had the honor of numbering among his disciples a great artist, Jusepe Ribera, who carried Ribalta's ideals to their supreme expression.

RINCON, Fernando del (?-after 1518).

This unassuming painter, a Castilian and contemporary of Pedro Berruguete, has reaped the benefit of having a legend attached to his name. Old writers, from the time of Butron, Carducho and Pacheco (17th century), persistently mention an Antonio Rincón, painter to their Most Catholic Majesties, who was the first artist in Spain to break with the Gothic style and use "rounded forms and better proportions, in closer conformity to nature" (Cean Bermudez). Actually no such Antonio Rincón ever existed, and his celebrity is due to a series of mistakes. The only painter named Rincón at the time of their Most Catholic Majesties was Fernando del Rincón of Guadalajara who, after the death of Queen Isabella in 1504, was appointed to be a kind of Superintendent of Painters and Painting in Castile during the reign of King Ferdinand. There is some recorded information about him, beginning in 1491 when he was at Saragossa with the Aragonese artist Martin Bernat and continuing to 1518, when his name is associated with that of the sculptor Philip de Vigarney (or de Bourgogne) at Alcala de Henares. Meanwhile he worked in the Cathedral of Toledo with other artists, among them Jean de Bourgogne and Frutos Flores. The portrait of Francisco Fernandez de Cordoba in the Prado and an important panel from San Francisco de Guadalajara, the *Martyrdom of Saints Cosmas and Damian*, are ascribed to him.

SERRA, Jaime (?-ca. 1395/96) and Pedro (?-after 1405).

The Serra brothers carried on the strain of Sienese tradition introduced by Ferrer Bassa and are the dominating figures of Catalan painting in the second half of the 14th century. Apart from meager references to their studio, nothing is known of their lives and most of their works have disappeared. Jaime, the elder brother, was director of the studio. His name is first mentioned in 1361 in connection with the only work unquestionably his that remains to us, an altarpiece for the tomb of Fray Martin de Alpartil, Canon and Treasurer to the Archbishop of Saragossa. No further mention of him is made after 1376; he seems to have died about 1395-1396. His brother Pedro, who may have been born in 1343, is referred to in 1363 as Jaime's collaborator. Five years later we find him painting independently. His chief work is the large altarpiece of the *Holy Spirit* in the Cathedral of Manresa (1393-1394). Also attributed to him is the altarpiece of the *Mother of God*, done for the Monastery at Sigena, now in the Museum of Barcelona. Pedro Serra is mentioned again in 1405. There was a third and younger brother, Juan, also a painter, but none of his work is known. Mention is also made of an uncle, who was banished from Barcelona and sought refuge at Valencia.

YANEZ DE LA ALMEDINA, Hernando (?-1536) and DE LLANOS, Hernando (?-after 1525).

These two painters, both of Castilian extraction and both born in La Mancha, worked in the Cathedral of Valencia between 1506 and 1513. There they collaborated (1507-1509) on a large-scale work, the decoration of the doors of the High Altar with a set of paintings illustrating the *Life of the Virgin*. These pictures, in which Leonardo's influence is very marked, show that the artists had come directly in contact with North Italian painting. When the document revealing the painters' names came to light not long ago it was remembered that a certain 'Ferrando espagnolo' was one of Leonardo's assistants when, in 1505, he was at work on the *Battle of Anghiari* for the Signoria at Florence. But which of the two Hernandos was it who worked with Leonardo? Probably it was Yañez to whom this honor fell. His was the more powerful personality of the two and his painterly background, at once more solid and more varied, accounts for his greater originality. Ascribed to him, among the pictures in Valencia Cathedral, are *The Meeting at the Golden Gate, The Presentation of the Virgin, The Visitation, The Adoration of the Shepherds, The Resurrection, Pentecost, The Dormition;* the remaining works are probably by the hand of Llanos. After their collaboration at Valencia, the two artists parted company. Llanos settled in Murcia, where he worked in the cathedral and in neighboring churches. We can follow his activities up to 1525. All his life he remained a docile imitator of Leonardo; but his composition shows little skill and his drawing less. We find Yañez at Cuenca in 1526 where, that same year, he painted an altarpiece for the Chapel of the Albornoz in the Cathedral. He continued working in Cuenca Cathedral until 1531. The paintings by him in the Cathedral illustrate the evolution of his art; after having absorbed the lessons of Leonardo, Giorgione and the Venetians, Yañez attained a vigorous, original expression of his own, stamped with a characteristic Spanish realism. In addition to the works referred to above, other pictures by Yañez are in the Prado and the Museum of Valencia, where there is also a typical work by Llanos.

BIBLIOGRAPHY

This bibliography is confined to works that have appeared in book form. We have deviated from this only in the case of a few articles of exceptional interest and some which, published serially in periodicals, amount to full-length monographs. For a complete bibliography the reader is referred to the standard work on the subject: CHANDLER RATHFON POST, *A History of Spanish Painting*, Cambridge, Mass. 1930 etc. For good bibliographies see also: JUAN DE CONTRERAS, Marquès de Lozoya, *Historia del arte hispánico*, Barcelona-Buenos Aires 1931 etc.; E. LAFUENTE FERRARI, *Breve historia de la pintura española*, Madrid 1946; MATILDE LOPEZ SERRANO, *Bibliografia de arte español y americano*, 1936-1940, Madrid 1942.

EARLY WRITERS

Vicente CARDUCHO, *Diálogos de la pintura*, Madrid 1633; reprinted, Madrid 1865. — Francisco PACHECO, *Arte de la pintura*, Seville 1649; reprinted, Madrid 1866. — Jusepe MARTINEZ, *Discursos practicables del nobilísimo arte de la pintura* (edited by Valentin Carderera), Madrid 1866. — Fray Juan RICCI, *Tratado de la pintura sabia*, published in *La vida y la obra de Fray Juan Ricci*, by E. TORMO, C. GUSI and E. LAFUENTE FERRARI, vol. I, Madrid 1930. — A. A. PALOMINO Y VELAZCO, *El museo pictórico y escala óptica*, 3 vols., Madrid 1715-1724. Parts one and two were republished in 2 vols., Buenos Aires, Poseidon Press, 1944. Part three, *El Parnaso* (lives of the Spanish painters and sculptors), was reprinted in the *Fuentes* of Sánchez Cantón, vol. IV (see below). — Antonio PONZ, *Viaje por España*, Madrid 1772 etc. — Juán Agustín Ceán BERMÚDEZ, *Diccionario histórico de los más ilustres profesores de las Bellas Artes en España*, 6 vols., Madrid 1800. A supplement to this Dictionary was published by Count de la VIÑAZA, *Adiciones al Diccionario de D. Juán Agustín Ceán Bermúdez*, 4 vols., Madrid 1894. (Deriving from the works of Palomino and the Dictionary by Ceán Bermúdez, several abridgements and compilations were issued under various titles in the 18th century and at the beginning of the 19th, in English, French and German. These works, however, made no new contribution to the subject.)

SOURCE BOOKS AND DOCUMENTATION

F. J. SÁNCHEZ CANTÓN, *Fuentes literarias para la Historia del Arte español*, 5 vols., Madrid 1923-1941. — M. HERRERO GARCIA, *Contribución de la Literatura a la Historia del Arte*, Madrid 1943. — M. R. ZARCO DEL VALLE, *Documentos inéditos para la Historia de las Bellas Artes en España* (Colección de documentos para la Historia de España, vol. 55), Madrid 1870. — M. ABIZANDA Y BROTO, *Documentos para la Historia artística de Aragón*, Saragossa 1915-1917. — M. SERRANO Y SANZ, *Documentos relativos a la pintura de Aragón durante los siglos XIV y XV*, in *Revista de Archivos, Bibliotecas y Museos*, Madrid 1914-1917. — *Documentos para la Historia del Arte en Andalusia* (Laboratorio de Arte de la Universidad), Seville 1927 etc. — R. DE ARRELLANO, *Artistas de Córdoba* (Colección de Documentos para la Historia de España, vol. 107), Madrid. — *Notas del Archivo de la catedral de Toledo*, redactadas sistemáticamente en el siglo XVIII etc. (Centro de Estudios históricos), Madrid 1914. — *Datos documentales para la Historia del Arte español* (documents relating to the Cathedral of Toledo), 2 vols., Centro de Estudios históricos, Madrid 1914-1916. — J. ALLENDE SALAZAR and F. J. SÁNCHEZ CANTÓN, *Retratos del Museo del Prado*, Madrid 1919. — A. L. MAYER, *Meisterwerke der Gemäldesammlung des Prado in Madrid*, Munich 1922. — F. J. SÁNCHEZ CANTÓN, *Dibujos españoles*, 5 vols., Madrid 1930. — A. BARCIA, *Catálogo de la colección de dibujos originales de la Biblioteca Nacional*, Madrid 1906. — *Museo del Prado, Catálogo de los cuadros* (edited by F. J. Sánchez Cantón), first edition, Madrid 1933; since then periodically revised editions. For biographies of painters, see: *Allgemeines Künstler-Lexikon*, THIEME-BECKER, Leipzig 1907 etc. — J. GESTOSO Y PEREZ, *Ensayo de un Diccionario de los artífices que florecieron en Sevilla*, 3 vols., Seville 1899 - 1908. — C. LOPEZ MARTINEZ, *Arquitectos, escultores y pintores de Sevilla*, Seville 1928. — Baron DE ALCAHALÍ, *Diccionario biográfico de artistas valencianos*, Valencia 1903. — A. BAQUERO ALMANSA, *Catálogo de los profesores de Bellas Artes murcianos*, Murcia 1913. — R. RAMIREZ DE ARRELANO, *Catálogo de artéfices que trabajaron en Toledo*, Toledo 1920. — A. FURIÓ, *Diccionario histórico de los más ilustres profesores de las Bellas Artes en Mallorca*, Palma 1839.

Chief periodicals dealing with Spanish art: *Boletín de la Sociedad española de Excursiones*, Madrid; *Boletín de la Sociedad castellana de Excursiones*, Valladolid; *Archivo español de Arte y Arqueología*, Madrid; *Archivo español de Arte*, Madrid; *Arte español*, Madrid; *Anales y Boletín de los museos de Arte de Barcelona*; *Archivo de Arte valenciano*.

GENERAL

L. VIARDOT, *Notice sur les principaux peintres de l'Espagne*, Paris 1839. — E. HEAD, *Handbook of the History of Spanish and French Schools of Painting*, London 1848. — W. STIRLING, *Annals of the Artists of Spain*, 3 vols., London 1848. — J. D. PASSAVANT, *Die christliche Kunst in Spanien*, Leipzig 1853. — E. LAFORGUE, *Des arts et des artistes en Espagne jusqu'à la fin du XVIIIᵉ siècle*, Lyons 1859. — L. VIARDOT, *Les Musées d'Espagne*, Paris 1862. — P. DE MADRAZO, *Viaje artístico de tres siglos por las colecciones de cuadros de los Reyes de España*, Barcelona 1884. — C. BLANC, *Histoire des peintres. Ecole espagnole*, Paris 1886. — P. LEFORT, *La peinture espagnole*, Paris 1893. — K. JUSTI, Introduction to 'Baedeker' (1st edition, 1900). — N. SENTENACH, *La pintura en Sevilla*, Madrid 1902; English edition: *The Painters of the School of Seville*, London and New York 1911. — C. GASQUOINE HARTLEY, *A Record of Spanish Painting*, London 1904. — K. JUSTI, *Miscellaneen aus drei Jahrhunderten spanischen Kunstlebens*, 2 vols., Berlin 1908. — E. BERTAUX, *Exposición retrospectiva de arte. Texto histórico y crítico* (in Spanish and French), Saragossa 1908. — E. BERTAUX, Chapters on Spanish painting in *Histoire de l'Art*, directed by A. Michel, Vol. III/2 (1908) and Vol. IV/2 (1911); continued in following volumes by P. PARIS. — C. H. CAFFIN, *The History of Spanish Painting*, New York 1910. — A. L. MAYER, *Sevillaner Malerschule*, Munich 1911. — M. DIEULAFOY, *Espagne et Portugal*, Paris, 'Ars Una.' — A. DE BERUETE, *Spanish Painting*, London 1921. — V. VON LOGA, *Die Malerei in Spanien vom 14. bis 17 Jahrh.*, Berlin 1923. — A. L. MAYER, *Historia de la pintura española*, 2nd edition, Madrid 1942 (ed. revised after the Spanish Civil War). — H. KEHRER, *Spanische Kunst vom Greco bis Goya*, Munich 1926. — *Spanish Art*, in *Burlington Magazine Monographs II*, London 1927. — P. PARIS, *La peinture espagnole*, Paris 1929. — C. R. POST, *A History of Spanish Painting*, Cambridge, Mass. 1930 etc. — Juan DE CONTRERAS, Marquès de LOZOYA, *Historia del Arte Hispánico*, 5 vols., Barcelona-Buenos Aires 1931-1949. — Enriqueta HARRIS, *Spanish Painting*, London 1938. — P. JAMOT, *La peinture espagnole*, Paris 1938. — J. GUDIOL, *Spanish Painting*, Toledo, Ohio, 1941. — E. LAFUENTE FERRARI, *Breve Historia de la pintura española*, 3rd edition, Madrid 1946. — M. SERULLAZ, *Evolution de la peinture espagnole*, Paris 1947. — P. GUINARD and J. BATICLE, *Histoire de la peinture espagnole* (from the 12th to the 19th century), Paris 1950.

ROMANESQUE PAINTING
(12th and 13th centuries)

J. PIJOAN, *Les pintures murals catalanes*, Barcelona (Institut d'Estudis Catalans). — W. W. S. COOK, *The Earliest Painted Panels of Catalonia*, series of articles in *Art Bulletin*, 1922-1928. — G. RICHERT, *Mittelalterliche Malerei in Spanien, Katalanische Wand- u. Tafelmalereien*, Berlin 1925. — J. FOLCH Y TORRES, *Museo de la Ciudadela, Catálogo de la sección de arte románico*, Barcelona 1926. — J. GUDIOL Y CUNILL, *La pintura mig-eval catalana. Els primitius*, 2 vols., Barcelona 1927-1929. — G. ROUCHÈS, *La peinture espagnole, Le moyen âge*, Paris 1927. — C. L. KUHN, *The Romanesque Mural Painting of Catalonia*, Cambridge, Mass. 1928. — A. L. MAYER, *El estilo románico en España*, Madrid 1931 (German edition, 1928). — C. R. POST, *A History of Spanish Painting*, vol. I, Cambridge, Mass. 1930 (complete bibliography up to 1930). — Ayuntamiento de Barcelona, *Museo de Bellas Artes. Frontales románicos*, Barcelona 1944. — W. W. S. COOK and J. GUDIOL RICART, *Pintura y imagineria románicas*. Historia universal del arte hispanico, vol. VI, Madrid 1950. — R. DEL ARCO, *La pintura mural en Aragón* and *El real monasterio de Sigena*, in *Boletín de la Sociedad española de Excursiones*, 1921 and 1924.

THE PRIMITIVES
(14th and 15th centuries)

(J. GUDIOL Y CUNILL), *Catálogo del Museo arqueológico-artístico episcopal de Vich*, Vich 1893. — S. SANPERE MIQUEL, *Los cuatrocentistas catalanes*, 2 vols., Barcelona 1905-1906. — E. BERTAUX, *Les primitifs espagnols*, series of articles in *La revue de l'art ancien et moderne*, 1906-1909. — E. BERTAUX, Chapters on Spanish painting in *Histoire de l'art*, directed by A. Michel, vol. III/2 (1908) and vol. IV/2 (1911). — J. GUDIOL and S. SANPERE MIQUEL, *La pintura mig-eval catalana (Els trecentistes*, Barcelona 1924. — A. L. MAYER, *El estilo gótico en España*, Madrid 1929. — A. DURAN Y SANPERE and others, *La peinture catalane à la fin du moyen âge*, Paris 1933. — J. GUDIOL RICART, *La pintura gótica a Catalunya*, Barcelona 1938. — J. GUDIOL RICART, *Historia de la pintura gótica en Cataluña*, Barcelona, n.d. (1944?). — M. TRENS, *Ferrer Bassa i les pintures de Pedralbes* (Institut d'Estudis Catalans), Barcelona 1936. — J. GUDIOL Y CUNILL, *El pintor Lluis Borrassa*, Barcelona 1925. — J. GUDIOL RICART and J. AINAUD DE LASARTE, *Huguet*, Barcelona 1948. — M. BETI, *El arte medieval del Maestrazgo. El pintor cuatrocentista Valentin de Montoliú*, Castellon 1927. — B. ROWLAND, *Jaime Huguet*, Cambridge, Mass. 1932. — J. AINAUD DE LASARTE and F. P. VERRIÉ, *El retablo del altar mayor del monasterio de San Cugat del Vallés y su historia*, in *Anales y Boletín de los museos de Arte de Barcelona*, 1941. — E. TORMO, *Levante* (Guías regionales Calpe), Madrid 1923. — E. TORMO, *Un museo de primitivos. Las tablas de las iglesias de Játiva*, Madrid 1912. — E. TORMO, *Valencia, Los Museos*, Madrid 1932. — J. SANCHIS SIVERA, *Pintores medievales en Valencia*, Valencia 1930. — E. TORMO, *Jacomart y el arte hispano-flamenco cuatrocentista*, Madrid 1913. — TRAMOYERES, *Un colegio de pintores*, Madrid 1912. — TORMO, *Rodrigo de Osona, padre e hijo, y su escuela*, in *Archivo español de Arte y Archeologia*, 1932-33. — L. DE SARALEGUI, *Pedro Nicoláu* and *El maestro de los Marti de Torres*, in *Boletín de la Sociedad española de Excursiones*, 1941 and 1942. — L. DE SARALEGUI, *El maestro de Santa Anna y su escuela*, Valencia 1949. — M. MANCHEÑO Y OLIVARES, *Una joya artística desconocida* (frescos in the Church of Santa Maria, Arcos de la Frontera), Seville 1917. — J. POLO BENITO, *Las pinturas murales de la capilla San Blas de la catedral Primada de Toledo*, Toledo 1925. — J. MARTIN MONSÓ, *Estudios histórico-artísticos (relativos principalmente a Valladolid)*, Valladolid 1893-1901. — J. E. DIAZ-JIMENEZ, *Catedral de León. El retablo*, Madrid 1907. — F. J. SÁNCHEZ CANTÓN, *Maestro Nicolas Francés, pintor* and *Tablas de Fernando Gallego en Zamora y*

Salamanca, in *Archivo español de Arte y Archeologia*, 1925 and 1929. F. J. SÁNCHEZ CANTÓN, *Maestro Jorge Inglés, pintor y miniaturista del Marqués de Santillana*, in *Boletín de la Sociedad española de Excursiones*, 1917. — E. TORMO, *Bartolomé Bermejo*, in *Archivo de Arte y Archeologia*, 1926. — J. GESTOSO, *Pintores sevillanos primitivos*, in the periodical *Museum*, 1918-1920. — J. HERNANDEZ DÍAZ, A. SANCHO and F. COLLANTES, *Catálogo monumental de la provincia de Sevilla*, Seville 1939-1943. — J. HERNANDEZ DÍAZ and A. SANCHO, *Los Reyes catolicos y la capella de San Gregorio en Alcala del Rio, estudio de una pintura mural*, Seville 1939.

THE RENAISSANCE
(16th century)

F. J. SÁNCHEZ CANTÓN, *Mito y realidad de Rincón, pintor de los Reyes catolicos*, in the periodical *Las Ciencias*, 1934. — C. GAMBA, *Pietro Berruguete*, in the periodical *Dedalo*, 1927. — R. LAINEZ, *Pedro Berruguete, pintor de Castilla*, Madrid 1935. — HULIN DE LOO, *Pedro Berruguete et les portraits d'Urbin*, Brussels 1942. — D. ANGULO, *Pedro Berruguete en Paredes de Nava* ('Obras maestras del Arte español'), Barcelona 1946. — E. TORMO, *Desarrollo de la pintura española en el siglo XVI*, in *Varios estudios de arte y letras*, Madrid 1902. — J. GUDIOL Y CUNILL, *Mestre Joán Gascó*, Barcelona 1908. — J. RAMÓN DE CASTRO, *La pintura en Navarra en el siglo XVI*, San Sebastian 1934. — R. CHABÁS, *Las pinturas del altar mayor de la catedral de Valencia*, Valencia 1891. — M. GONZÁLES MARTÍ, *Las tablas de los pintores Llanos y Almedina del siglo XVI*, in the periodical *Museum*, 1914-1915. — María-Luisa CATURLA, *Ferrando Yañez no es Leonardesco*, in *Archivo español de Arte*, 1943. — E. TORMO, *Valencia. Los Museos*, Madrid 1932. — A. IGUAL UBEDA, *Juan de Juanes*, Barcelona 1943. — D. ANGULO, *Artistas andaluses: Alejo Fernandez* (Laboratorio de arte de la Universidad), Seville 1946. — D. ANGULO, *Alejo Fernandez, Los retablos de D. Sanchez de Matienza, de Villasona de Mena*, in *Archivo español de Arte*, 1943. — E. TORMO, *El Divino Morales*, Barcelona 1917. — D. BERJANO ESCOBAR, *El pintor Luis Morales (El Divino)*, Madrid 1922. — L. ROBLOT-DELONDRE, *Portraits d'Infants*, Paris-Brussels 1913. — A. BERUETE, hijo, *Los pintores de Felipe II*, in *Conferencias de Arte*, Madrid 1924. — P. ZARCO, *Pintores españoles en San Lorenzo de El Escorial* (1566-1613), Madrid 1931. — P. ZARCO, *Pintores italianos en San Lorenzo de El Escorial*, Madrid 1931. — F. DE SAN ROMÁN, *Alonso Sánchez Coello (ilustraciones a su biografía)*, Lisbon 1938. — F. DE SAN ROMÁN, *Juan Pantoja de la Cruz*, Madrid 1921. — F. M. TUBINO, *Pablo de Cespedes*, Madrid 1868. — R. HUGUET, *Los cuadros del pintor Francisco Ribalta existentes en Castellón*, Castellón 1913. — TORMO, *La educación artística de Ribalta*, in *Revista critica hispano-americana*, 1916. — L. TRAMOYERES BLASCO, *Los pintores Francisco y Juan Ribalta*, in *Archivo de Arte valenciano*, 1917. — D. F. DARBY, *Francisco Ribalta and his School*, Cambridge, Mass. 1938. — J. MARIA DE ASENSIO Y TOLEDO, *Francisco Pacheco, sus obras artísticas y literarias*, Seville 1867. — H. F. COOK, *Pacheco, the Master of Velazquez*, in the *Burlington Magazine*, 1907. — F. RODRÍGUEZ MARÍN, *Francisco Pacheco, maestro de Velazquez*, Madrid 1923.

EL GRECO

S. VINIEGRA, *Catálogo ilustrado de la esposición de las obras de Dominico Theotokopuli, llamado el Greco*, Madrid 1902. — M. B. COSSIO, *El Greco*, 2 vols., Madrid 1908; reprinted in 1 vol. (without illus.), Buenos Aires 1944 (Colección Austral). — A. F. CALVAERT and C. GASQUOINE HARTLEY, *El Greco, an Account of his Life and Works*, London 1909. — F. DE SAN ROMÁN, *El Greco en Toledo* (documents), Madrid 1910. — MEIER-GRAEFE, *Spanische Reise*, Berlin 1910. — Maurice BARRÈS, *Greco ou le secret de Tolède*, Paris 1912. — A. L. MAYER, *El Greco, Eine Einführung*, etc., Munich 1911, 3rd ed., 1920. — G. BERITENS, *Aberra-*

ciones del Greco cientificamenta consideradas, Madrid 1913. — R. Jorge, *El Greco, Nova contribução biografica, critica e medica de estudo do pintor Dominico Theotocopuli*, Coimbra 1913. — M. Utrillo, *Domenikos Theotokopulos 'El Greco,'* Barcelona n.d. — P. Lafond, *Le Greco, sa vie, son œuvre*, Paris 1913. — E. Tormo, *Los medicos y el caso del Greco*, in 'Por el Arte', Madrid 1913. — A. de Beruete, *El Greco, pintor de retratos*, Madrid 1914. — H. Kehrer, *Die Kunst des Greco*, Munich 1914. — G. Beritens, *El astigmatismo del Greco*, Madrid 1914. — R. Domenech, *La casa del Greco*, Barcelona 1914. — Miguel de Unamuno, *Le Greco*, in 'Rassegna del Arte', Rome 1914. — I. L. Melida, *Significación del Greco en la pintura española*, Madrid 1914. — I. L. Melida, *El arte antiguo y El Greco*, Madrid 1915. — L. Venturi, *La formación del estilo del Greco*, in 'Boletin de la Sociedad española de Excursiones', 1918. — M. Dvorak, *Ueber Greco und den Manierismus*, in *Kunstgeschichte als Geistesgeschichte*, Munich 1924. — A. L. Mayer, *El Greco* (with a critical catalogue), Munich 1926. — F. de San Román, *De la vida del Greco* (Nueva serie de documentos), Madrid 1927. — Willumsen, *La jeunesse du peintre El Greco*, 2 vols., Paris 1927. — E. H. del Villar, *El Greco en España*, Madrid 1928. — J. A. Merediz, *La transformación española de 'El Greco'*, Madrid 1930. — F. Rutter, *El Greco*, London 1930. — A. L. Mayer, *El Greco*, Berlin 1931. — J. Cassou, *Le Greco*, Paris 1931. — A. Kyrou, *Domenikos Theotokopoulos krees* (in Greek), Athens 1932. — C. Mauclair, *El Greco*, Paris 1934. — A. Bertram, *El Greco*, London 1934. — J. Goyanes, *El Greco pintor místico*, Madrid 1936. — Alexandra Everts, *El Greco*, Madrid 1936. — M. Legendre and A. Hartmann, *Dominico Theotokopuli dit El Greco*, Paris 1937. — A. Busuioceanu, *Les tableaux du Greco dans la collection royale de Roumanie*, Paris-Brussels 1937. — *Dominico Theotocopuli El Greco. Exposition organisée par 'La Gazette des Beaux-Arts'* (Catalogue edited by Assia Rubinstein, assisted by A. Busuioceanu and A. L. Mayer. Texts by G. Wildenstein, A. Busuioceanu, A. L. Mayer, R. Cogniat). — R. Pallucchini, *Il Politico del Greco della R. Galleria Estense* (R. Istituto d'Archeologia e Storia dell'Arte. Opere d'Arte), Rome 1937. — R. Escholier, *El Greco*, Paris 1937. — D. Talbot Rice, *El Greco and Byzantinism*, in the *Burlington Magazine*, 1937. — Eugène Dabit, *Les maîtres de la peinture espagnole, Le Greco, Velazquez*, Paris 1937. — L. Goldscheider, *El Greco*, Phaidon Press 1938. — H. Kehrer, *Greco als Gestalt des Manierismus*, Munich 1939. — K. Pfister, *El Greco*, Zurich 1941. — E. Waldmann, *Domenicos Theotokopulos genannt El Greco*, Bielefeld-Leipzig 1941. — C. de Lasterra, *El sentido clasico en El Greco*, Madrid 1942. — M. Gomez Moreno, *El Greco*, Barcelona 1943. — M. Gomez Moreno, *El entierro del Conde de Orgaz* ('Obras maestras del arte español'), Barcelona 1943. — Maria L. Caturla, *La Veronica. Vida del tema y su transformación por El Greco*, Madrid 1944. — J. Babelon, *El Greco*, Paris 1946. — Jean Cocteau, *Greco*, Paris 1944. — El Marquès de Lozoya, *El San Mauricio del Greco* ('Obras maestras del arte español'), Barcelona 1947. — G. Grappe, *El Greco*, Paris 1948. — J. Camón Aznar, *Dominico Greco*, 2 vols., Madrid 1950 (this work brings together all the known material relating to El Greco, with a new catalogue of his paintings and nearly 1000 illustrations). — Elizabeth Du Gue Trapier, *The Son of El Greco, Notes Hispanic*, New York 1943.

INDEX OF NAMES

THIS,

THE SIXTH VOLUME OF THE COLLECTION

PAINTING ○ COLOR ○ HISTORY

WAS PRINTED

BOTH TEXT AND COLORPLATES

BY THE

SKIRA

COLOR STUDIO

AT IMPRIMERIES RÉUNIES S.A.,

LAUSANNE

FINISHED THE FIFTEENTH DAY OF APRIL

NINETEEN HUNDRED AND FIFTY-TWO

PRINTED IN SWITZERLAND